Wild Duck
and their pursuit

Wild Duck
and their pursuit

DOUGLAS BUTLER

MERLIN UNWIN BOOKS

First published in Great Britain by Merlin Unwin Books, 2010

Published by:
Merlin Unwin Books Ltd
Palmers House
7 Corve Street
Ludlow
Shropshire SY8 1DB
U.K.

www.merlinunwin.co.uk

The author asserts his moral right to be identified with this work.

Designed and set in Bembo by Merlin Unwin
Printed in Great Britain by TJ International, UK
ISBN 978 1 906122 24 9

Contents

To Patricia

ACKNOWLEDGEMENTS

Without the help of many people these pages would never have seen the light of day. First of all my thanks to my sons Rupert and Paul, and to John Condon, Philip Walsh, Michael Gately, Anthony O'Halloran, Michael Meaney and to numerous other shooting companions. Together we have shared the magic of the changing light on marshes, bogs, foreshore, flight ponds and stubbles. To that shared magic this book owes its origins.

I owe a special debt of gratitude to Professor John O'Halloran of University College Cork for an invaluable discussion on population dynamics. Also to Dr John Harradine of BASC for his helpful advice on alternatives to lead shot.

Michael Hanley, Agricultural Specialist with the United States Department of Agriculture and Andrew D. Taylor, Wildlife Officer with the Canadian Wildlife Service, provided me with a positive mass of information on hunting regulations in their respective countries. My thanks to both of them.

To George Lett of Wexford a very special thank you for taking me out punt gunning on his beloved Wexford Harbour. George is a master of his art and has an encyclopaedic knowledge of punt gunning.

Last but by no means least, I must record my thanks to Merlin and Karen Unwin for their unfailing courtesy and help.

Douglas Butler
July 2010

Photographic acknowledgements

The publishers wish to thank the author for supplying the majority of the photos in this book. However, the following people have also kindly helped provide photographs (relevant page numbers given after subject).

David Mason (wildlife photographer): pochard 52, ruddy duck 37, pochard 216-7, and the great jacket photos of mallard and teal.

Nicholas Cottrell (Wildfowl & Wetlands Trust, Slimbridge): teal 39, tufted 39, pochard 129, tufted 129. **James Lees** (WWT): pochard 39.

Alan D. Wilson at Nature's Pics (www.naturespicsonline.com): green-winged teal 39.

INTRODUCTION

For the genuine sportsman there is a passion inextricably linked to his chosen pursuit. It is a passion likely to exceed all reason and one which has its origins in some strange mix of psyche, culture, nationality and other less readily-identifiable entities. It is a passion that blinds him, almost inevitably, to the delights of other sports even those most closely related to his own. Take what is generically called football. In Britain football can only mean the 'Beautiful Game' (though men of the Welsh valleys who tend to think of a game with a different shaped ball may take issue with this). In Ireland it means 'Gaelic Football' and, on the other side of the earth, a grandson of Gaelic Football called 'Australian Rules'.

A similar diversity is to be found amongst those of us who, gun in hand, pursue the creatures of the wilds. For one man the sport is all about tall pheasants skilfully presented over deep and rugged valleys. To another it is all about a gentle potter along autumn hedgerows in search of rabbits and an occasional pheasant. And to yet another, especially if he is lucky enough to live along the western fringes of Britain and Ireland, it is all about putting in the hard miles across rough covers and bogs in pursuit of woodcock and snipe.

Even amongst those whose passion is fuelled by the flight of the wild ducks, there can be firmly held views as to what their sport is really all about. To some the focus is on wild and windswept salt marshes with the ever-present roar of the sea and the whistling of wigeon cocks in the dark sky. To others everything revolves around flight ponds. Dug out many years ago and lovingly tended, they provide those delicious moments on a winter's evening when the music of mallard wings and the piping of teal fill the air in the gathering gloom.

There are those who ply their trade beyond the sea wall who refer to their sport as wildfowling. This is to distinguish it from the duck shooting that takes place inland. To the aficionado there is a real difference though, I must confess, it is not one to which I subscribe. To me there is little difference between flighting the wigeon packs over mudflats and over flooded water meadows many miles from the sea — although I have no difficulty in accepting that others may have strongly held views to the contrary.

Life in these early years of the 21st century imposes upon us demands that rarely crossed the minds of sportsmen of past generations. All important — we have to be conservationists. Indeed we must be better conservationists than those who glibly claim such title but do precious little about it. To this end we need to know a great deal about the birds that we hunt and the factors which impinge upon their populations. We need, too, to have a sound realisation of the fragility of the natural world so that we can ensure that our activities do not threaten its wellbeing. For these reasons I have, without apology, in a book about duck shooting, devoted the early chapters to the ducks themselves and to their ways.

Before embarking upon this story I want to return to the analogy that I drew with football. When young men from the ancient universities of Oxford and Cambridge toured America to play rugby in the late 1800s, little did they realise that they were sowing the seeds of a very different game. A game similar in objective but alien in substance. In similar vein, duck hunting in North America has developed its own different and unique traditions. The sheer vastness of the continent, the needs of pioneering peoples and the incredible numbers of migrants that wing south each autumn have all conspired to mould that different tradition. I have therefore thought it worthwhile to include sections on the ducks of North America and the hunting scene there.

Opposite page: Domesticated mallard — the heavier farmyard type

CHAPTER ONE

FIRST ENCOUNTERS

Little more than a generation ago most people were familiar with the common breeds of domestic fowl. Even the inhabitants of upmarket, leafy suburbia were likely to see hens and ducks in the course of their weekend jaunts into the countryside. The more knowledgeable could probably even distinguish between Light Sussex, Rhode Island Reds and the other types of farmyard hen. Geese, too, were a not unfamiliar sight in rural parts. They would be seen passing the summer months grazing contentedly in grassy fields and growing fat enough to make a more than adequate dinner for farming families from September onwards.

Then there were the turkeys. In the Tipperary countryside of my childhood, many a cottage acre would be adorned with a dozen or two. In those days it was the custom to build cottages on acre plots. With this amount of land it was reckoned that the occupiers could reach a fair degree of self-sufficiency in respect of vegetables. Those turkeys were destined to do wonders for the cash flow of their owners at Christmas. They were real bronze turkeys, the colour that Nature had ordained for them in their native America. Guinea Fowl were also common in that era. I recall one village in which every second cottage seemed to have a flock of them. They used to spend much of their time on the road and it was only a comparative lack of cars that allowed them to adopt such a carefree lifestyle. If they were around today the carnage would be massive. Nowadays my only brush with them is in upmarket eateries where they grace the menu with such exotic creatures as ostriches, swordfish and kangaroos. We simply did not appreciate what we had in those far-off days.

More people than ever before now live in a greatly extended and rather less than leafy suburbia. Farmyards today are rarely graced by chickens and are effectively devoid of ducks. Turkeys are confined to a relatively small number of enormous flocks which, mostly, never see the light of day. The corollary of all this is that the average child of the 21st century may never come face to face with a hen or duck in what may be termed a traditional setting. Indeed the same child's most likely first encounter with these feathered friends may well be in the pets' corner of a zoo or in some twee and folksy theme park. In both cases long-suffering parents will likely have paid some astronomical sum for the privilege of exposing their offspring to the domesticated members of the avian persuasion.

Should that child, by some perverse fluke of luck, encounter a domesticated duck or, for that matter, a hen or a turkey, in some forgotten rural backwater, it will almost certainly be white. Mankind, and equally womankind (we must not be sexist) appears to have decreed that the fowl that we breed to eat or to provide us with eggs should be of this colour. Whether there is any logic in this selection is a moot point. Why, it is reasonable to ask, should we opt for a colour which, with a handful of exceptions, Nature has rejected other than for certain denizens of high altitude where it serves as camouflage? Completely white birds of any species are, in these islands, comparative rarities. In the world of wild ducks, despite countless meetings, I have only once or twice come across a truly wild bred one. This is in contrast to the situation on shoots where large numbers of captive bred birds are released. Down the years I have seen hundreds of thousands of pink-footed geese in the morning sky. On only one occasion did a skein contain a white one.

There are those who attempt to justify the selection of white-feathered poultry on the basis that the flesh is superior in terms of flavour and texture or because they have superior growth rates. I have, however, yet to see incontrovertible scientific evidence in favour of such propositions. I am reliably informed that that doyen of the culinary arts, one Mrs Beeton, held the view that birds with white feathers put in a superior performance on the table. My personal experience is very much to the contrary. Accepting that many of one's childhood experiences are viewed through rose-tinted spectacles, there is no doubt in my mind that the big red cockerels that roamed our farmyard were infinitely more tasty than the 'plastic' oven-ready offerings of today which are all the same size and which lie in neat rows in supermarket freezer cabinets. Equally, the predominantly brown ducks that waddled out to the fields in the early morning and returned faithfully to the yard at sunset were much more succulent than their latter-day white-feathered counterparts which find their way into the Chinese restaurants of every provincial town.

My personal belief is that the quest for whiteness has little to do with anything other than the age-old association with purity and cleanliness. For example, rats bred for research and dissection are invariably white. White mice are obtainable in every pet shop. I suspect that mothers are just about prepared to tolerate these little rodents in the house as pets if they are white as opposed to the more usual mouse colour. If I am correct in my belief then the selection of white for the modern domesticated duck is based upon total misconception.

Whatever their colour, ducks are undoubtedly the muckiest of domesticated birds. They like nothing better than a prolonged paddle in the softest and dirtiest mud. White or brown, it makes no difference. Then there is the matter of their diet. If we were sensitive souls we might think twice about consuming a bird that likes nothing better than a feed of juicy slugs and snails. Again, white or brown it makes no difference.

Paradoxically the aforementioned inhabitants of not too leafy suburbia probably have a better chance of seeing a wild duck than a domesticated one. Here I refer specifically to mallard, the most ubiquitous of all the species of wild ducks. Very many human habitations developed along river banks, courtesy of the Vikings and other like-minded land grabbers and, despite the rather less than pristine quality of river water at the present day, few rivers, even in the heart of great cities, are without their complement of mallard. Whether it is the Thames in London, the Clyde in Glasgow or the Liffey in Dublin, there are few stretches from which mallard are absent. Equally, there can be few ponds or lakes in town parks without a few pairs. Wild, it has to be admitted, is not always the most appropriate adjective to describe these particular mallard. In the absence of persecution they tend to become the most trusting of birds, coming readily to accept whatever scraps of food a human benefactor has on offer. Despite this, however, even the most apparently 'tame' mallard are apt to display a vestige of their wildness. After a day spent relaxing on water in close proximity to humankind, they are quite likely to take wing at dusk and seek out some lonesome nocturnal feeding spot. Stand by any river in a town towards the end of the day and you will see them begin to move, often in quite surprising numbers. And this despite the fact that they have, almost certainly, been well fed by locals on and off throughout the day.

Aside from mallard, wild ducks can vary quite considerably in the degree of tolerance which they display in the face of human presence. Some of this has to do with location and some to the nature of the birds themselves. In a town park, for example, other wild duck can become

Mallard at Marlfield Lake, Tipperary, where they demonstrate the least fear of man of any duck species.

quite tame, though not all species to the same degree. There will be those that, like mallard, will come to accept food whilst others will display a rather greater reserve. Partly for this reason people with no more than a passing interest in wildfowl may be able to name a few species and yet not even recognise the names of others.

Not so long ago I was watching a re-run of a popular quiz show on television. The contestant had breezed through the earlier questions and had displayed a fine range of general knowledge. He had reached the level of very serious prize money, about half a million pounds if memory serves me correctly. Then came THE question. What manner of creature is a merganser? Not, to my mind, a particularly difficult question but clearly one that underlined how little most people know about ducks. The contestant did not know the answer and the question-setter was proved correct in assigning the question to this level of perceived difficulty. In fairness though, I suppose that it should be said that there are not too many town parks graced by a pair of mergansers.

It is possible to assess the relative wariness of the different duck species by careful observation of an area of water which is subjected to regular human presence. A medium-sized lake is ideal, one which supports a good mixed wintering population of duck. Marlfield lake on the outskirts of Clonmel in county Tipperary is such a place. A public road with parking facilities runs along one side and here the ducks are a popular attraction. The far side is wooded, fringed with a good range of vegetation, and is for practical purposes inaccessible. The lake is over two hundred yards wide so the various species of ducks have ideal opportunity to express their relative affections for the human race. Due to regular feeding by visitors, mallard, as usual, are quick to spot a potential benefactor and congregate on the roadside in quite large numbers. Not infrequently they are joined by coots, aggressive birds which quickly lose their fear of man. Though slightly more reticent, tufted duck come almost up to the water's edge when food is on offer. They appear to be wintering in ever-increasing numbers on urban and suburban waters and seem to enjoy an easy relation-ship with us. However, they display a tiny touch of reticence and only rarely join mallard on the bank. Their close relative, the pochard, is a rather less trusting customer and usually keeps some distance out from the bank. I have yet to see one coming to accept a handout but maybe they do so in some places.

Gadwall, like tufted duck, can grow quite tame though never to the same degree as mallard. There are sometimes in excess of a dozen pairs on Marlfield lake. Some, when food is thrown in, will join the mallard but they are quick to dart away if there is any sudden movement. They can be surprisingly aggressive and, despite their smaller size, have no problem with making a drive at any mallard that has the temerity to steal their piece of food. But not all of them display the same degree of tolerance of human presence. Some have a habit of cruising up and down twenty yards or more out and only approaching the bank when humanity departs.

Shoveler usually have little time for people or their offerings. Their clear preference is to remain well out on open water. At Marlfield their numbers build towards seventy or eighty as autumn progresses. They spend their days sleeping and dabbling on weed beds that cover shallows well away from the road.

As a general rule teal and wigeon tend to harbour grave suspicions concerning human intent. Of the two, teal are the more likely to adopt a conciliatory mode in response to regular human presence. A few pairs

Pintail (above) and wigeon — two of the more timid species of wild duck.

6

Loch Ryan, a sea loch near Stranraer.

come across to the road but they are quick to seek the sanctuary of open water if one attempts to approach them. But, judging by the intensity of their piping, most of the teal at Marlfield seem happier when safely positioned near the far bank. This is where the wigeon congregate. They hardly ever come across the lake. The same holds true for the very occasional pintail that puts in an appearance.

Whilst wigeon rarely lose their inherent wildness, there are places in which they will just about tolerate a human observer as long as he does not attempt to get too close. I know of a number of sheltered bays with a road running nearby where they grow used to passing traffic. If, though, a car should stop and the occupants emerge, they will usually lift and then alight some fifty or one hundred yards further out. One of my favourite spots for watching newly-arrived wigeon is just outside Stranraer where the A77 runs along the bank of Loch Ryan. The considerable number of cars passing to and from the port, most of which do not stop at this time of year, have engendered a degree of familiarity in the wigeon. During October their numbers build up as the month progresses and they are usually to be seen bobbing up and down at the tide's edge. Most times they are in the company of smaller numbers of mallard and tufted duck. There are often a few eiders and scaup there as well.

So, somehow, somewhere, man makes his first contact with ducks. It is, invariably, a sympathetic contact if for no better reason than they are birds that it is impossible to dislike. Magpies can irritate with their non-stop, noisy chatter, ravens have ominous associations of mortality, vultures look quite appalling. But ducks press all the right buttons. Their plumage is attractive, their flight is a model of aeronautical precision, they waddle disarmingly and they produce large broods of fluffy ducklings. And, all important, they do the cat thing. Park mallard, which are most people's interface with the duck world, come rushing up in the expectancy of being fed. We know perfectly well that their interest in us is simply and solely confined to a perception that we are purveyors of food. But we kid ourselves that, like pussy, they have formed some indefinable emotional attachment.

At this juncture, for the great majority of people, matters go no further. Ducks are nice but they are only a minuscule part of the natural world and all that it has to offer. If anything humanity now subjects itself to a serious collective bout of anthropomorphism. Donald Duck, Jemima Puddle Duck and a host of other personified ducks now become the main occupants of the quacking world. But, for a tiny minority of us, those same first contacts were the beginning of a passionate affair almost certainly destined to last a lifetime. Somewhere deep in our psyche a hunting instinct bequeathed by distant ancestors is sired by these strange and beautiful birds and by thoughts of their wild and lonesome haunts. It is an instinct that will force us to leave our beds at unearthly hours whilst saner mortals slumber on. It is an instinct that will compel us to travel to windswept sea lochs and mudflats. And it is an instinct which commands our presence on marsh or foreshore when white clouds stream across the moon on a winter's night.

CHAPTER TWO

ABOUT DUCKS

We share our planet with a quite extraordinary range of creatures. Each of them occupies its own special niche in the overall scheme of Nature. In order to understand where wild ducks slot into this great spectrum of life it is necessary to probe a little into taxonomy, the branch of biology which deals with classification. Without some form of pigeonholing, a study of the natural world would be next to impossible. Essentially the taxonomist divides the living world into groups, subgroups, sub subgroups and so on. As this division proceeds, the relationship between members of subgroups becomes increasingly more pronounced. In classical biology the process of grouping is based primarily upon anatomical features. As a case in point our relationship to the orang-utan and the chimpanzee is self-evident. Now, with our exploding knowledge of DNA, the closeness of these relationships has been brought even more sharply into focus. As the division into subgroups proceeds, the proportion of common DNA increases quite dramatically.

Biologists used to divide the great array of life into two kingdoms: plant and animal. However, this became rather less than satisfactory when it became apparent that very many organisms did not sit happily in either of these kingdoms. Consequently most biologists now think in terms of five kingdoms of life. Only the animal kingdom concerns us here.

Animals are organisms which sustain themselves by consuming other organisms either directly, as we do, or indirectly, by assuming a parasitic lifestyle.

The first division of a kingdom is into broad groups called phyla. Our focus is confined to the most advanced phylum, the Chordata. Along with ourselves and the other mammals, the Chordata embraces birds, reptiles, amphibians and fish. These apparently diverse life forms are bound together by a number of basic features. In particular they possess a backbone (which is cartilaginous rather than bony in some of the primitive fish such as sharks and rays), a tubular nervous system that runs through the backbone and, at some stage of the life cycle, gill slits. Yes, surprisingly, for a brief period, you, I and ducks possessed the respiratory apparatus of aquatic creatures.

At this juncture humans and ducks go their separate ways. A phylum is divided into classes, five in the case of the Chordata. Ducks belong to the class Aves which includes all birds. They share with mammals the luxury of being warm blooded. This means that they can get on with life without being troubled by external temperature fluctuations, unless they are very extreme. Birds and mammals retain heat generated in their bodies by use of two insulators: fat and air. The fat lies in deposits of varying thickness beneath the skin. Feathers, like hair, are cleverly designed to trap a layer of air next to the skin. When external temperatures drop, both structures can be erected in order to hold more insulating air.

So ducks belong to the phylum Chordata and the class Aves. The sub subgroup is called an order. The class Aves is divided into a number of orders. What we commonly refer to as 'wildfowl', and what our American colleagues call 'waterfowl', form an order with the quite atrocious name of Anseriformes – literally birds whose body shape approximates to that of a goose. In other words we are talking of ducks, geese and swans. As well as having broadly similar anatomical features, they are characterised by a predisposition towards living in watery places. The order also contains a very small numbers of very unusual birds called screamers. They are confined to South America and need not concern us.

An order is in turn divided, this time into families. Ducks, geese and swans by way of distinction from the screamers form the family Anatidae.

We have now reached the stage of sub sub subgroup. The next division is into genera (genus in the singular). The geese that grace Britain and Ireland fall into one of two main genera. The grey geese belong to the genus Anser and the black geese to the genus Branta. There are several genera of ducks but, as we shall see, those that we hunt fall mainly into two of these.

Defining the duck

Ducks are readily distinguished from geese and swans by a number of features. Primarily most of them are smaller. Their necks are much shorter, a feature which is most clearly visible when they are in flight. On water, when relaxed, they adopt a somewhat hunched appearance with the head sunk onto the body so that the neck may not be visible at all. However, at the slightest hint of danger the head comes up and the elegant neck of their kind is revealed. As a general rule ducks have narrower and more pointed wings than geese and swans and in flight the wing beat is faster. A pronounced feature of all ducks is their flattened bill. Close observation reveals that it is covered by a soft, thin skin. In most species the bill ends as a hard tip called the nail. Not surprisingly, since they spend a considerable amount of time in contact with water, ducks possess a thick, waterproof

Mallard drake entering eclipse   *Greylag geese*

plumage. Beneath this is a dense layer of down which traps sufficient air to insulate them from the coldness of the water.

During flight wing feathers come under considerable pressure as they propel the bird through the air. This is especially true of fast flying birds like ducks which frequently cover long distances in the course of a single flight. As a result they must spend a considerable amount of time taking care of their feathers. Watch them after a period of feeding. Preening, as the activity of feather care is called, involves careful reconstruction of feathers using the bill and, to a lesser extent, the sides of the head.

Oil is an essential requirement for this restorative work. It is secreted by a stumpy gland on the back at the base of the tail called the preen gland. It is especially obvious in a plucked mallard. The duck pulls on the gland with its bill to stimulate it to release oil. In all birds the oil helps to keep the feathers supple and in good order. In wildfowl, in addition, it serves the vital task of waterproofing. If a lot of duck are concentrating on a small body of water it is not unusual to see a film of preen oil on the

Mallard preening: an essential activity which repairs and oils the feathers in readiness for both flight and swimming.

surface. In my experience it is especially evident on flight ponds that are being fed regularly. The ducks come in at dusk, gorge themselves and then get down to a serious bout of preening.

Like the hair of mammals, feathers have a limited life and must be replaced at regular intervals. As a prelude to this replacement, the old feathers must be moulted. Wildfowl are unusual in that they lose all their flight feathers at the same time. In consequence they become flightless for a few weeks each year.

Elsewhere in the avian world, flight is not sacrificed during the moult as only a few of the flight feathers are replaced at a time. Ducks are clearly more predator-prone during this flightless period. As a result they tend to spend their days well out on open water or skulking in dense aquatic vegetation.

In Western Europe wild ducks begin their moult as the breeding season draws to a close. Their young, though not yet able to fly, are by now becoming more independent and in less need of parental care. For mallard the moult usually begins towards the end of June and is well in evidence in July. There can though be quite a lot of variation in relation to the start of the moult. Early this morning, 21 April, I was feeding a flight pond (we try to keep birds around as much as possible during the close season by offering a very limited supply of barley.) It works quite well and unpaired drakes in particular come to take advantage of our largesse.

At the edges of the pond were a few bundles of chestnut feathers, the first indication of the forthcoming moult. For teal the moulting period is much the same as for mallard. But for late breeders, especially tufted ducks, it usually starts rather later in the summer.

Male and female plumage differences

One of the many attributes of wild ducks is the variety and splendour of their plumage, especially that of the males. In most species the sexes are readily distinguishable and for some the differences are quite dramatic. The mallard drake is a case in point with his glossy green head, white collar and silvery back; a very different creature from his dowdy partner. Equally, male wigeon, teal and pintail possess striking plumages. All three have silvery grey backs and brightly coloured heads. In wigeon and teal the head is chestnut, veering slightly to orange. The former has a yellowish buff forehead and the latter a green stripe around and behind each eye. But, of them all, the pintail drake takes pride of place with its chocolate coloured head adorned by an eye-catching white stripe on either side.

In some duck species there is a brightly coloured wing patch called the speculum. It is present in both sexes and is most commonly green or blue, sometimes tinged with an additional colour.

Females camouflaged for incubation

The difference in colour between the sexes is worthy of comment. Nature has endowed the females with a mixture of browns in recognition of their need to be suitably camouflaged. They are, in the main, ground nesters and it falls to them alone to incubate the eggs. This requires them to remain on the ground for a considerable period, three weeks for example in the case of teal. The larger mallard eggs will take a further week to hatch. Without a plumage which blends them into the background they would quickly fall prey to foxes, stoats and other predators that roam far and wide in search of a tasty meal. Their partners, being absolved of this particular component of domestic endeavour are not subject to the same restrictions. Essentially their brightly coloured plumage is a secondary sexual character which, like the flowing mane of a stallion, promotes their cause when going about the important business of being taken seriously by a prospective mate.

Eclipse plumage

When the moult comes in summer, the males lose their finery and grow what is called their eclipse plumage. Except at close range they are now effectively indistinguishable from their partners. They will remain like this until a new plumage is grown in the autumn. Eclipse plumage makes excellent sense. There are obvious dangers attendant upon being brightly coloured whilst flight is not an option and predators are rarely far away. And anyway, the ladies of the species have no interest in them at this time of year.

Both within and between species there can be considerable varia-tion in the amount of time taken to acquire a new plumage. When the shooting season starts in September few mallard drakes are fully coloured. There is also the question as to whether the first drakes in the bag are first year birds which have not yet acquired their finery or adults emerging from eclipse. The colour of the legs and paddles is probably the best guide at this time of year. In first year birds, they are yellow-orange; whereas in adults they are bright orange. As September gives way to October an increasing proportion of drakes have acquired full plumage and most will have completed the transition before November. In my experience wigeon and teal tend to be a little slower and it is not uncommon to shoot males of these species in late autumn which are still some way short of full plumage. Shoveler can be even slower. I have shot birds in December which had still not acquired their full range of colours.

Whereas geese and swans pair for life, ducks typically only pair for the forthcoming breeding season. In the case of mallard the bond is usually firmly established by December though it can be much earlier. I

A female mallard showing her camouflaged plumage which usually blends perfectly into the grass and ground foliage in which she nests.

can recall occasions whilst flighting in November when, having shot a single bird from a high pair, I have witnessed the return of the partner within minutes. It will circle calling for its mate and is likely, in those less cautious moments, to provide one with another opportunity.

Nesting places

Most mallard nest on the ground, often a considerable distance from water. The chosen site is likely to be in heavy cover at the base of a hedge or under a bush. Occasionally they will opt for a more elevated site such as the head of a pollarded willow which may be ten or twelve feet above the ground. Just outside Cambridge lies a local beauty spot. In times past (I cannot vouch for the present) it used to be frequented by what were politely referred to as courting couples. The mallard here tended to nest in trees, an excellent example of Natural Selection. Ground level activity in the area was so intense that the birds genetically programmed to nest on the ground rarely succeeded in raising a brood. In contrast, their tree-nesting brethren, free from the threat posed by amorous humanity, could bring forth their young in peace and so pass on this valuable trait. The ducklings eventually tumbled down from the trees unharmed.

Nesting season

Mallard mostly start laying in March though it is not unusual to find clutches in February, especially if the month turns mild. In Ireland, in particular, the proximity of the Atlantic engenders such mildness. But many of these early clutches are destined to come to an untimely end. February is probably the hungriest month of all for predatory creatures and there is rarely sufficient foliage to provide adequate concealment for eggs. Carrion and hooded crows take a serious toll at this time of year. Magpies, too, are especially fond of large, yolky duck eggs. Should those early clutches escape the roving eyes of egg thieves there is yet another hurdle to be negotiated. Young birds of all species require large quantities of the protein rich bodies of insects if they are to make that rapid and demanding transition to adulthood. February eggs produce March ducklings and, unless the weather is on the balmy side, there is an almost inevitable shortage of these all-important insects.

Mallard drakes losing their breeding finery.

Number of eggs in a clutch

In common with birds such as partridges and pheasants, ducks tend to lay large numbers of eggs. For mallard a clutch of between eight and twelve is usual but even more are not uncommon. Most years I come across at least one family of fourteen or fifteen tiny ducklings. Last spring a brood of nineteen appeared on a small lake near here, one of the biggest that I have ever come across. Teal produce clutches of similar size to mallard but wigeon tend to lay fewer eggs, seven or eight being usual. Ducks rarely produce a second clutch other than in those situations in which the first one was lost, most likely as a result of predation. In my experience a second clutch of mallard eggs rarely exceeds six or seven.

A female mallard keeps close to her young clutch which are extremely vulnerable to predation in the early days.

Duckling predation

On emerging from the egg the young of some ground-nesting birds are much more advanced than the naked young which hatch in the deep security of an elevated nest. This extra degree of development has to be fuelled and, in consequence, ducks and their like lay proportionately larger eggs. When the ducklings emerge they are covered with a generous layer of down. Within a few hours they have dried off and immediately set about the all-important business of feeding themselves. Tiny bundles of non-stop motion, they rely initially upon their mother's preen oil to keep them buoyant. Their days are spent darting across the water in search of insects. At first they stay close to their mother but as time passes they forage over an ever-widening area. It is during these early days of a duck's life that one witnesses Nature at her most severe. A positive array of predators lie in wait. Pike, mink, crows and a host of others take their toll. I have seen a pair of hooded crows sweep down time and time again and snatch small ducklings from the water. Within days of hatching, healthy broods of nine or ten are likely to be reduced to something under half these numbers.

Behaviour of drakes

As we have seen, the drake takes no part in the tedious business of incubation. Whilst his mate is putting in the hard hours, he may be seen in the general vicinity of the nest. Or, there again, he may desert her and join up with a group of unpaired drakes. These drake packs are a common sight in late spring, especially in areas where mallard are plentiful. They are frequently in the air and will relentlessly pursue any duck that has the misfortune to come to their attention. Ducks that have left their eggs for a short period in order to feed are particularly at risk. Should one take to the air to escape these unwelcome attentions she will in all probability be forced down again. The drakes will then attempt to mate with her. These pursuit flights are called 'reihen' and may culminate in the duck being drowned. Because of this untoward behaviour it makes very good sense to get rid of as many surplus drakes as possible towards the end of the shooting season. Unpaired drakes are quite simply a nuisance and, if at all plentiful, can cause serious disruption during the breeding season.

Even when incubation is over, the majority of drakes do little in the way of tending the brood. Some may be seen accompanying the duck and young but, more often than not, they leave that arduous duty to their partners.

Species give rise to new species

Altogether there are in excess of 140 species of ducks, geese and swans on earth at the present day. It is not possible to be more precise because a species is not an immutable grouping. In different parts of its range, the environment places different demands on the individual members. The result is that local populations tend to emerge which are uniquely equipped to cope with the particular requirements of their own patch. As time passes, these local populations gradually grow more different from one another. Essentially it is the nature of a species to break up into what are called geographical races.

Initially these emerging subdivisions of a species are likely to be very similar. This is demonstrated by the fact that individuals from different races can interbreed successfully. With the passage of a lot more time the races grow increasingly dissimilar until, in taxonomic terms, they are afforded the title of subspecies. It is not possible to decide precisely when this transformation takes place. Indeed the question of whether the component segments of a species are geographical races or have evolved further to the level of subspecies is often the subject of heated academic debate. In the fullness of time the subspecies themselves, through ongoing specialisation, will eventually become sufficiently different to merit the title of species. As was the case when trying to decide at which point races diverge sufficiently to become subspecies, there is equal difficulty in deciding when subspecies diverge sufficiently to be recognised as separate species.

An example of the subdivision of a species in Britain and Ireland is to be found in the whitefronted goose which breeds on the tundra across almost the entire northern hemisphere. Experts differ as to whether there are four or five races/subspecies. No matter, only two concern us here. One of these subspecies winters in England and Wales (and in continental Europe) and the other in Ireland and western Scotland. The English/Welsh birds originate in Siberia whilst the Irish/Scottish ones come from Greenland. What is unusual is that these two subspecies, widely separated as breeding populations, all but overlap on their wintering grounds. Most years a handful of the Greenland race turn up in Wales and a similar tiny number of the Siberian race appear in Ireland.

To a greater or lesser extent every species is at some point along this evolutionary road. Hence the difficulty in deciding precisely how many species of wildfowl presently inhabit the earth.

Dabblers and divers

In both Britain and Ireland, duck hunters confine their attentions to a limited number of species. Less than a dozen are legitimate quarry at present. According to their feeding habit they can be divided into two groups: dabblers and divers. The dabblers, namely mallard, gadwall, teal, wigeon, pintail and shoveler belong to the genus Anas. The principal divers on the quarry list are pochard, tufted duck and scaup. They belong to the genus Aythya. Scaup are hunted in Ireland but not in Britain. For the average duck shooter, dabblers almost invariably constitute by far the greater proportion of the bag.

Dabbling ducks feed on and beneath the surface of shallow waters. Most people are familiar with the sight of upending mallard, tail pointing skywards and body half submerged. Some dabblers also feed by grazing. It is not uncommon, for example, to see wigeon packs on grassy fields from which floodwaters have recently subsided. They may well be in the company of geese or swans. To a lesser extent than wigeon, gadwall will sometimes be seen grazing. Other than in the manner of their feeding, dabbling ducks exhibit a number of features which distinguish them from their diving cousins. In terms of plumage there are two such features. First there is the difference between the sexes. In dabblers it is far more pronounced. Then there is the brightly coloured spectrum of which mention has already been made. It is only present in dabblers.

In all ducks the legs are set rather far back on the body. This gives rise to the characteristic waddle of their kind. Nature did not intend ducks to

Gadwall – a dabbler which, in common with the wigeon, will sometimes graze. *Scaup – a diver, only a handful of which breed in Britain every year.*

be high speed performers on land, especially divers whose legs are set back even further than those of dabblers. This adaptation provides the propulsion for efficient swimming underwater. Nevertheless, a wounded duck can on occasions provide one with a fair run.

One other difference between the two groups has special relevance when it comes to shooting. Without exception, dabbling ducks can rise from the water with considerable acceleration when disturbed. Teal in particular are renowned for the challenge provided by their ascent. Strictly though, there is not a great deal of difference between teal and other dabblers when it comes to speed of getting airborne. Even the shoveler, often wrongly thought of as being clumsy on account of its outsize bill, is no slouch. In contrast the diving ducks – with one exception, the goldeneye – cannot lift directly from water. They need a take-off run, rather after the manner of moorhens and coots, in order to get into the air.

Some ducks spend the greater part of their life at sea and only deign to come inland during the breeding season. Most of these so-called sea ducks are no longer hunted here. Goldeneye and scaup are the only exceptions on this side of the Atlantic. During the winter one is unlikely to meet scaup inland other than when the weather is very stormy. Goldeneye are small, fast flying ducks which, like scaup, dive to feed on small molluscs and other marine invertebrates. They are more inclined than other sea ducks to venture inland. Up to 5,000 have been counted on Lough Neagh in Northern Ireland and thousands are regularly present on the Firth of Forth. At dawn, goldeneye are often the first ducks on the wing. Before it is light enough to see them, their presence overhead is betrayed by a strange humming wing beat very different from that of other ducks. Goldeneye were formerly only winter visitors to Britain but some are now remaining to breed. The first recorded occurrence of breeding was in Cheshire in 1931.

Duck species in North America and Britain and Ireland

In the USA, the variety of wild ducks pursued by North American hunters provides an intriguing illustration of the vagaries of Nature. Once again dabblers and divers find their way into the bag. But as well as these, a variety of sea ducks and sawbills can be hunted. In order to make comparison with the quarry species of Britain and Ireland it is convenient to divide the ducks of the New World into five groups.

1. Ducks that belong to the same species that occur in Britain. These are ones that enjoy widespread distribution across the northern hemisphere.
2. Ducks of the same species as in Britain but which belong to different races or subspecies. Once again we meet the vexed question of race versus subspecies.
3. Ducks which are quite obviously similar to ones occurring in Britain but which belong to different but closely related species.
4. Ducks that have no British equivalents.
5. Ducks that are no longer hunted in Britain.

1. Ducks belonging to the same species that occur in Britain

Pride of place here must go to the ubiquitous mallard. Found right across the northern hemisphere, this most resilient of birds has been successfully introduced into New Zealand, Australia and Hawaii, mainly from Britain. No other duck in the world is in the same league when it comes to ease of breeding captive stock and releasing the progeny. Worldwide many millions are released by hunters each summer. In Britain alone an estimated 500,000 are released annually. North American mallard are slightly smaller than their European counterparts. Otherwise they are virtually identical so that, despite the size difference, the two populations are regarded as being of the one race. A number of different races are found in the southern hemisphere. For the great majority of duck hunters the mallard is likely to be the major component of their annual bag.

Second only to the mallard comes the pintail, another species which breeds from Alaska in the west, right across to the far eastern extremes of Asia. Like the mallard, its world population is numbered in millions. Strictly we should call it the northern pintail in order to distinguish it from a number of closely related species, in particular the yellow-billed pintail which is widespread in the southern half of South America.

Two other dabblers fall into the present category: the gadwall and the shoveler. The former, like mallard and pintail, breeds over a vast area of the North American continent but generally a little further south. The latter is equally widely distributed. Strictly, as with the pintail, we should refer to the northern shoveler. This is necessary as there are a number of other shovelers, all of which are confined to the southern hemisphere.

Finally there is the ruddy duck, a native of North America. It is not indigenous to Europe but an expanding population in Britain has now extended into Ireland. It has also spread to the European mainland where it was first recorded breeding in France in 1988. The ruddy duck is an example of a truly accidental introduction of an alien species. First brought to the wildfowl collection at Slimbridge in Gloucestershire in 1948, escapees quickly laid the foundation of the present population. Its recent appearance on the quarry list in both Britain and Ireland has little to do with officialdom's desire to improve our sport and a lot to do with a hope that it will be exterminated. This is because it has an unfortunate habit of hybridizing with the rare white-billed duck. This is a species found mainly in eastern Europe but there is a small, isolated population in Spain. Concern for the genetic purity of these birds is the sole reason that the ruddy duck has been consigned to the firing line.

2. Ducks of the same species as in Britain but which belong to different races or subspecies

In terms of numbers bagged each season, the teal comes second only to the mallard in both Britain and Ireland. As it has a close relative in North America we shall, for present purposes, refer to it as the European teal. This close relative, the green-winged teal, is exactly the same in size but the males are just sufficiently different in plumage to warrant being placed in a separate subspecies. It can be distinguished from the European teal by a conspicuous white stripe on either side of its breast. The females however are effectively indistinguishable.

Every autumn a small number of green-winged teal manage to stray across the Atlantic, no mean feat considering the distance involved and the fact that they weigh at most around 350 grams. They are greatly assisted in this arduous journey by the prevailing westerly winds. But I often wonder if any of them make it back – a few thousand miles into a more than stiff head-wind must be a daunting prospect. Each autumn an average of about ten appear in Ireland where it has now been recorded in fourteen counties. It must be remembered however that there are a number of extensive wildfowl collections in Britain so that there is always a possibility that a sighting is of an escapee rather than a genuine trans-Atlantic vagrant.

Two species of scaup are found in North America, the greater and the lesser. The greater scaup belongs to the same species as the British bird but is assigned to a different race on account of its slightly smaller size and darker colour. There is no equivalent to the lesser scaup in Britain. In appearance it closely resembles the greater scaup but is smaller and the males have a small tuft on the back of their heads.

Another diving duck, the goldeneye, is found right across the northern hemisphere. As with the greater scaup there are slight differences between the North American and British birds. This time it is the American birds that are slightly larger. Once again the differences are just about sufficient to merit a division of the species into races. Another species, Barrow's goldeneye, which is similar in appearance but larger, is also found in North America. Small numbers of these birds breed in Iceland but strangely, considering that many wildfowl of Icelandic origin winter in Britain and Ireland, they do not condescend to visit our shores. A third species of goldeneye, the diminutive bufflehead, is also hunted in North America.

Ruddy duck.

Bufflehead.

3. Ducks which are obviously similar to ones occurring in Britain but which belong to different yet closely-related species

Number one in this category is the American wigeon, or Baldpate, as it is affectionately known. Slightly larger than our wigeon, the male's white forehead and green-banded face betray little of its close relationship to the European wigeon. But the familiar whistling confirms the kinship. Also, the American wigeon, like its counterpart in Britain and Ireland, favours broad expanses of shallow water where it can dabble and graze. The females of the two species are quite similar but, as a general rule, there is more greyish brown in European birds and more rufus brown in the American ones. Like the green-winged teal, the American wigeon has a habit of straying across the Atlantic. In his book *Birds of Ireland*, Clive Hutchinson details 26 appearances in the Ireland between 1966 and 1989. Of these the most dramatic was surely a pack of 13 seen in Kerry in 1968. Once again though there is the proviso that some of these birds may have escaped from wildfowl collections.

So while some ducks may cross the Atlantic with the help of a tail wind, it is even more extraordinary that the European wigeon crops up as an annual wanderer in North America. Writing in 1901, George Bird Grinnell, the famous duck hunter and author, comments in his book *American Duck Shooting* that it is a frequently-seen straggler in North America. He further states that it breeds in Alaska but I can find no evidence in support of this. He also records them being shot in places as far apart as California, Illinois, Pennsylvania and Florida. He himself shot a European wigeon in North Carolina. Some of these birds may indeed have been genuine trans-Atlantic vagrants. The great majority though, I suspect, were of Asiatic origin, as the species breeds right across the northern reaches of that continent as far as the Pacific coast. In fact it would probably be more accurate to call the European wigeon the Eurasian wigeon.

The two species of wigeon, Eurasian and American, provide further insight into the evolutionary process. Here, quite clearly, we have the break-up of an ancestral species into new ones. Whilst retaining many common features, the two populations have, through isolation from one another, grown steadily different.

Some European species and their closely-related American counterparts

European wigeon

American wigeon

European teal

Green-winged teal (US)

Pochard

Redhead (US)

Tufted duck

Ringneck (US)

To those living in Britain and Ireland, the diving duck that we most closely associate with North America is undoubtedly the canvasback. At a distance its whitish body, black breast and chestnut head betray its close relationship with the pochard. Like the pochard it is usually to be seen in rafts, sometimes in the company of other diving ducks, well out on open water. Also like the pochard, the canvasback engages in a pattering take-off run across the water surface but, once airborne, is an equally strong flyer. At close quarters the heads of the two birds are seen to be quite different. That of the pochard is rounded whereas that of the canvasback comes to something of a peak and then slopes forward into a rather longer bill. The females of the two species are broadly similar. In size the canvasback is a little bigger than the pochard.

A second close relative of our pochard is the redhead. Slightly smaller than the canvasback it shares its distinctive plumage and enjoys a similar distribution across North America. The redhead is, if anything, more pochard-like in that its head is rounded and in size it is only marginally larger.

Our second major diver, the tufted duck, also has an equivalent species in North America. This is the ring-necked duck. Its name is not particularly apt as the collar that prompts its name is anything but easy to see other than at very close range. Both species are medium-sized and have a slightly dumpy appearance. The most obvious distinguishing feature of the males is the colour of their flanks: white in the case of the tufted duck, and silver grey in the ring-necked duck. As well as this, the European tufted duck possesses the extravagant tuft of head feathers which give it its name.

4. Ducks that have no British equivalent

There are a number of species in this category. We have already met the lesser scaup. Of the remainder, four in particular are much sought-after by American hunters. They are the American black duck, the blue-winged teal, the cinnamon teal and the wood duck.

The American black duck is closely related to the mallard, so closely in fact that hybrids between the two species are encountered quite commonly. In size and general shape it is very like the mallard but in plumage it is very distinct. Unusual amongst dabbling ducks there is little difference between the sexes. Both are best described as blackish brown versions of the mallard. The black duck is one of the most common wildfowl species in the eastern United States. It has a particular fondness for flooded woodland. Two other mallard-like species are also hunted. They are the mottled duck and the Mexican duck, both somewhat similar in plumage to the female mallard. The mottled duck is found mainly in coastal regions of Florida and Texas, and south into Mexico. The Mexican duck, it would appear, is hybridizing with mallard, just like the black duck. In recent years it has been extending its range in some of the southern states.

Like the green-winged teal, the blue-winged teal is very widely distributed in the United States. The male is easily identified by its grey head and conspicuous white crescents in front of each eye. Female teal of all species tend to be dowdy creatures and quite similar to one another. In the case of the blue-winged teal, the female shares with her partner the blue forewing which affords the species its name and which is quite diagnostic. Most years small numbers succeed in getting lost during the autumn migration and end up in Britain and Ireland where they occasion great excitement amongst the twitching fraternity. Quite closely related is the cinnamon teal, a species easily identified by the bright rusty brown plumage of the male. The cinnamon teal generally occupies a more southerly range than the blue-winged teal but the ranges of the two species overlap, particularly in the western United States.

The hole-nesting wood duck has long been a popular quarry of

Cinnamon teal

Wood duck or Carolina

hunters. Such was its appeal that by the early years of the 20th century numbers had declined alarmingly. This fact was recognised when the United States and Canada agreed the Migratory Bird Convention in 1916. Article IV of the Convention awarded special protection to the wood duck and to another threatened species, the eider duck. The contracting parties agreed that this special protection should take the form of a shooting moratorium of at least five years or the establishment of reserves or such other regulations that would assure the future of the two species. The strategy proved successful and the wood duck population made a reasonably good recovery. Numerous attempts have been made to acclimatize this most attractive of ducks in Britain but sadly they appear to have met with little success.

This is in marked contrast to the fate of the wood duck's only close relative, the equally colourful mandarin. Brought to Britain from China, probably around the middle of the 18th century, the mandarin is now well established as a breeding species. The population is presently thought to be in excess of a thousand pairs, more in fact than are to be found in the whole of China. In his book *The Ark in our Midst* Richard Fitter records that the first reported shooting of a mandarin in Britain was at Cookham in Berkshire in 1866.

A strange-looking duck, the Fulvous whistling duck, or Fulvous tree duck, is another species hunted in some of the southern states of America. Whistling ducks are a group of tropical ducks with a quite distinctive appearance. They have much longer legs than any of the ducks hunted in Britain and Ireland. On land, whistling ducks are readily identified by their very upright stance.

Finally, there is the appropriately named Harlequin duck. This brightly-coloured small diving duck spends most of its life on coastal waters but moves inland to breed. It is protected in some parts of North America and hunted in others. There is, for example, an open season in British Columbia.

5. Ducks that are no longer hunted in Britain

These are predominantly sea ducks and sawbills. Scoters are black or predominantly black sea ducks which have not been hunted on this side

Common Eider (male) – once shot and farmed for its down, but now one of the species of sea duck protected in Britain and Ireland

of the Atlantic for many years. Two species, the common or black scoter and the velvet or white-winged scoter are found on both sides of the ocean. A third species, the surf scoter, which is easily recognised by the male's brightly coloured bill and white head patches, is confined to North America. As well as the scoters there are the eiders. Best known of these is the common eider which in times past was farmed for its down. Differences between British and American common eiders are just about sufficient to merit the acceptance of separate races. A number of other species of eiders occur in North America.

Then there is that most elegant of sea ducks, the long-tailed duck, also known in North America as the oldsquaw. This is a bird that spends a lot of its life well out to sea. In a fairly long life devoted to the pursuit of wildfowl I have only come across long-tailed ducks on a handful of occasions.

Last of all there are the sawbills. These are ducks that feed predominantly on fish and which, in consequence, possess serrated bills to secure their slippery prey. Two species are common to Britain and North America. Of the two the red-breasted merganser is the smaller. We call the larger one the goosander whilst our American colleagues refer to it as the common merganser. Because of their diet of fish they are anything but palatable. Quite recently a freshly shot (allegedly by accident) goosander was brought to me for identification. Despite its recent demise the smell was quite atrocious and I was left wondering why the sawbills are regarded as quarry by serious duck hunters. On the question of their edibility I was intrigued by a comment in the 2006/07 New York State hunting regulations. Mergansers, it stated, are the most heavily contaminated waterfowl species and should not be eaten. Mergansers are very unpopular with fishermen because of their habit of eating young salmon. It is permissible to shoot them in Scotland – under permit – for the protection of fish stocks. A third species, the smaller hooded merganser is confined to North America.

Ducks for Dinner

Finally, no description of the hunter's quarry would be complete without mention of its performance on the dinner table. After all, there would be precious little point in slaying these noble creatures of the wilds if they were not to be consumed.

As a general rule the taste and texture of meat reflects the feeding habit of the animal from which it is obtained. The flesh of herbivores is more palatable than that of carnivores unless, that is, a man demands 'strong meat'. For such a man I can heartily recommend scaup. Personally I give away the few that I shoot each season. The dabbling ducks, with the possible exception of shoveler, all make excellent eating. They feed predominantly on plant matter, almost exclusively in the case of wigeon. For choice I would always go for pintail and teal, and in that order. In my experience wigeon shot inland taste a lot better than ones shot on the coast. I have always attributed this to the fact that they are feeding on meadow grasses rather than marine vegetation which tends to make their flesh a little oily. The main diving species, tufted and pochard, are both omnivorous and the former in particular tends to have a high animal intake. Though not quite to the same extent as scaup, the result is meat which is most politely described as an acquired taste.

CHAPTER THREE

RESIDENTS, MIGRANTS AND THE NUMBERS GAME

In strict ornithological terms a bird qualifies as a resident if it is found in a particular country throughout the year and, all important, breeds in that country. For some species the entire population may be resident. Away from the world of ducks there is no better example than the red grouse. Few individuals stray very far from where they hatched and some spend their entire life in a relatively small area. As a general rule residents tend to stay put unless prompted to move by such factors as food scarcity or extreme meteorological conditions. In the case of quarry species a move to quieter pastures may be precipitated if hunting pressures become excessive.

When used in relation to birds, migration has a rather more precise meaning than that of everyday use. Specifically there is the implication that it is a regular event and one which is largely dictated by the changing seasons. There is the further implication that there will be a return to the region of departure. In relation to the migration of wildfowl in the northern hemisphere, movement is generally south in autumn with a return journey the following spring. Most rules have an exception or two. In Britain the small teal-like garganey provides one such. This little duck, like the swallow, comes to us from Africa each spring and has gone again by the end of October. This habit has earned it the country name of summer teal. I have only once encountered a garganey during the shooting season. Or, I suppose, to be more precise, on only one occasion was I aware that a particular small duck was a garganey and not a teal.

So far so good. The distinction between resident and migrant appears quite clear. Let us take a couple of examples. In Britain and Ireland the mallard is primarily a resident species – like the red grouse, large numbers are destined to spend their lives in the area in which they hatched. The mid-winter population however is boosted by migrants from mainland Europe. Some authorities claim both Britain and Ireland receive large influxes of these visitors. Whilst this is often the case for the counties of eastern England, it is not my experience in Ireland. In the various places in which I hunt I get a fair idea of the numbers of mallard present. I rarely if ever see any increase in winter other than during those increasingly uncommon periods of prolonged hard weather.

In contrast to mallard, the wigeon which we encounter in winter are almost exclusively migratory. Somewhere in the vicinity of 300,000 are present in Britain and Ireland by early December. Of these no more than about 500 are likely to be residents, nearly all of them in Scotland. In Ireland, breeding records can be counted on the fingers of a single hand.

For small countries, and in world terms many of the countries of western Europe are small or fairly small, it is a relatively simple matter to distinguish between residents and migrants. But let us now cross the Atlantic. In the United States the reality is that most wildfowl species are migratory *despite* the fact that countless individuals remain in the *same* country. October witnesses a massive movement of wildfowl in North America, indeed on a scale which is nothing less than breathtaking. From the vast breeding grounds of Alaska and the prairies of southern Canada and the northern United States quite extraordinary numbers pour south as autumn progresses. Take just one species, the blue-winged teal. These ducks begin to leave their breeding grounds in late August and by September migration is well underway. Somewhere in excess of 5,000,000 of them are on the move. Of these, despite a flight of thousands of miles, a considerable proportion will have never left the country of their origin. Residents or migrants?

The descent of wildfowl on Britain and Ireland in autumn is essentially the mass movement of whole populations or of significant segments of them. It is an evolutionary design which ensures that they have an adequacy of food during the winter months. Exactly the same holds true for North America. The movement is a response to the gradual freezing-over of the breeding grounds. Tucked away in the extreme north-west of Europe and bordered by the Atlantic, the island status of Britain and Ireland means that the winter harshness experienced in parts of mainland Europe is something of a rarity. What begins as a trickle of early arrivals in late August rapidly swells into a positive flood as the weeks of autumn pass. Before November has arrived, vast numbers of ducks, geese, swans and waders will have touched down at suitable locations along the shores of Britain and Ireland. Some of these will make the sheltered bays, the mudflats and the salt marshes their winter homes. Others will begin to move inland as the rising water table, fuelled by autumn rains, provides more and more suitable accommodation. Here they will stay until the early days of spring unless a prolonged period of frost drives them back to the milder surroundings of the coast. In Britain the greater part of the wintering wigeon population probably remains near the sea. Ireland is different. Its slow-flowing rivers with broad flood plains provide an almost unlimited quantity of suitable habitat. In consequence most Irish wigeon spend the winter miles from the sea.

Migratory routes of wildfowl

The study of ringed birds, or banded as they are referred to in North America, has proved invaluable in determining the migratory pathways of wildfowl. The ducks that visit Britain and Ireland in winter come from Iceland, almost all of northern Europe and still further east from the Siberian tundra. Some travel very long distances. Iceland is 600 miles away. Birds that come from far to the east face a journey of 2,000 miles or more. Wigeon come to us from Iceland to the west and from as far away as Siberia to the east. Those that appear along the west coast of Ireland in August and September are undoubtedly of Icelandic origin. Indeed Ireland is thought to be an important wintering area for this segment of the population. Teal, too, come from Iceland but the greatest numbers originate in Scandinavia and the Baltic States. Some of the teal that breed in Britain spend the winter in Ireland.

The North American continent is a vast land mass. An example may help to put things in perspective. That little duck mentioned earlier, the blue-winged teal, can engage in migratory flights of truly extraordinary lengths. Pride of place must surely go to one that was ringed in Manitoba and later recovered in Peru. It had flown a journey of around 4,000 miles to reach its wintering quarters.

Detailed studies of ringed (banded) recoveries in the United States revealed that wildfowl moving south follow one of four broad migratory routes. These routes and their associated wintering grounds are referred to as flyways. The four flyways, moving from west to east, are named Pacific, Central, Mississippi and Atlantic. In 1947 councils were set up for each of these flyways. They are composed, inter alia, of representatives of state and federal wildlife agencies. As part of their function, they collect

The administrative regions of the four waterfowl flyway councils in the United States of America

information concerning such matters as the levels of breeding success of the various wildfowl species and make recommendations for hunting regulations for the forthcoming season. Essentially their recommendations are an attempt to create a balance between the hunting harvest and the year's productivity. The result is an annual set of regulations which, to a European hunter, can look complex in the extreme. Daily bag limits, both total and for the various species, form an important part of these regulations. Some examples will be found in chapter eight.

Whilst the main autumn movement of wildfowl is effectively north-south, many duck species move on to more benign surroundings during periods of exceptionally harsh weather. Teal provide a good example, as they are especially sensitive to low temperatures. If a hard snap descends upon the mainland of Europe in mid-winter there is a significant influx of teal into Britain from the near continent. Should the hard snap persist and spread into Britain there is a further movement westwards into Ireland. Then, on those extremely rare occasions when Ireland experiences an extended

Blue-winged teal

period of low temperatures, teal move yet again. This time their destination is the Atlantic coast of France. Some may travel as far as Portugal. When the frost breaks they can be gone again in a flash. Over the years I can recall a number of occasions (though not many, because of the relative mildness of Irish winters) when at bedtime the mercury was well below the zero mark and there was clear promise of great things to come on the numerous small streams that grace this area. But in the night, the frost vanished and with it, the piping multitudes. In the dawn only a handful of slightly subdued snipe remained as a reminder of what could have been.

The arrival of the migrants

Few people are privileged to be in the right place at the right time to witness the arrival of large numbers of migrant wildfowl. There are a number of reasons for this. For a start they are likely to arrive during the hours of darkness. Then there is the fact that migratory flights of wildfowl tend to take place at high altitudes, birds only dropping low upon reaching a favoured bay or sea loch. But just once in a while one may be fortunate enough to come across a pack of ducks that have just touched down on a traditional roosting water on the way inland. In contrast one becomes much more aware that the return migration is getting underway in February and March. Rather like the swallows gathering in their hundreds on telephone wires as a prelude to their return to Africa, some duck species congregate in ever-increasing numbers in the days before they leave. This is most apparent in the case of visitors such as wigeon and teal. In Ireland, for example, large numbers of teal can be seen gathering on the river Brosna and its associated floodwaters as March progresses. Wigeon numbers too build up substantially in part of county Offaly prior to departure.

Other than the mallard there are few duck species with significant resident populations in either Britain or Ireland. The tufted duck, with an estimated breeding population of some 7,000 pairs for the two islands, comes in a poor second. Of these about 2,000 pairs occur in Ireland.

In passing I must note that I have always harboured serious reservations about published population estimates for both resident and migratory wildfowl. More on this later in the chapter.

Resident population numbers

There is little doubt in my mind that the resident population of tufted ducks in Ireland is expanding and at a substantial rate. Some thirty years ago conventional wisdom was that by far the greater part of the population was to be found in the north and west of the country. But nowadays I am meeting more and more breeding pairs in the southeast. Less than two miles from my home lies a bog with a central area of eleven or twelve acres of open water. Up to a decade ago we rarely met tufted ducks in the bog before mid-December. Then, gradually at first, numbers began to build in early spring. In 2007 there were several dozen present in early April and I encountered nine good broods later in the year. Strangely though, they do not seem to remain in the bog once the young can fly. When the shooting begins on 1 September there are only a handful left.

Not far behind tufted duck, in terms of resident numbers, comes the teal. The estimated breeding population for Britain and Ireland is between 3,500-6,000 pairs of which the majority are in Britain. It is claimed that no more than 1,000 pairs breed in Ireland. And, it is further claimed, this Irish breeding population is declining. This is a proposition with which I cannot agree, as all the evidence available to me points to the contrary. Teal are amongst the most secretive of nesters and I have only found the nest on rare occasions. However, a good gauge of breeding levels is the number of family parties encountered when the shooting season opens on 1 September. These are clearly not early immigrants as they show little inclination to leave the area even when there is substantial disturbance due to shooting. In the places in which I shoot there are always a few family parties about on opening day. Indeed I am now meeting them in places from which they were absent at this time of year less than a decade ago.

The UK and Ireland's only other duck to break the barrier of 1,000 breeding pairs is the shoveler. It is generally regarded as a scarce and somewhat erratic breeder, though I suspect, published figures once again seriously understate the real strength of the population.

Gadwall and pochard both breed here in limited numbers. Figures of a few hundred pairs for each species have been suggested. Gadwall are undoubtedly increasing in numbers in both Britain and Ireland. In 1850 a pair that had been caught in a decoy were released in East Anglia. It is

Pochard drake

thought that at least part of the present population is derived from this pair. Here in Tipperary we rarely saw more than the odd gadwall until a few years ago. Now they are breeding at a number of sites in the county. This year, for the first time, a pair appeared with a brood of eight on a lake just across the fields from my home. Pochard, too, are on the increase as a breeding species. Thirty years ago it was believed that no more than ten pairs bred in the whole of Ireland. They are now breeding in most counties. The published figure of 400 pairs for Britain and Ireland is, in my estimation, once again a definite understatement of the true position.

Of the remaining species on the quarry list, breeding numbers are very small. Between Britain and Ireland there are probably less than 200 pairs of the introduced ruddy duck and around 50 pairs of pintail. Goldeneye nest in holes in trees, something of a rare commodity in this day and age. They have been encouraged to nest in Scotland by the provision of nesting boxes. It is not unreasonable to suppose that similar success could be achieved in the Lough Neagh area in Northern Ireland by employing similar tactics.

North America experiences quite dramatic temperature extremes. Effectively this means that the wildfowl breeding grounds, which lie to a large extent in more northerly latitudes, become increasingly inhospitable as the breeding season approaches its end. Hence the vast southerly migration in autumn. Some species, and the blue-winged teal is once again an example, move far south to wintering grounds well removed from their breeding quarters. Other species such as the black duck tend to winter, at least in part, at the southern extremity of their breeding range. For yet other species the main population movement is south but some individuals can remain in northerly latitudes by taking advantage of the comparative mildness of the Pacific coast. The American wigeon, for example, can be found in winter along the coastline of southern Alaska and green-winged teal and shoveler in maritime regions of British Columbia. As indicated earlier it is for these sorts of reasons that it is a rather more onerous task to categorise North American wildfowl as migratory or resident than is the case with their equivalents in Britain.

We noted earlier that for both British and American duck hunters, the mallard is by far the most important quarry species. Whilst in North America the population is largely migratory, not inconsiderable numbers qualify as residents. This is due in part to widespread introductions for shooting. It is certainly a species which is disinclined to leave the area of its birth until it really has to. George Bird Grinnell records the fact that many wildfowl, and mallard in particular, remain in parts of the Rocky Mountains throughout the winter despite temperatures as low as -20°C or sometimes even −30°C. It is possible for them to do so where waters are sufficiently rough to prevent freezing. Likewise they remain in places where warm springs bubble up through the frozen earth and keep the frost at bay.

To a rather lesser extent the black duck population of North America is in part resident. The species is a great favourite with hunters of the eastern states, and local introductions, as in the case of mallard, have in places provided the basis of resident populations.

When the first settlers moved west, wild duck populations were of truly extraordinary size. There is little doubt that in those far off days some species were numbered in tens of millions. Inevitably though, as time passed, the combined effect of drainage of vast areas of the prairie breeding grounds and the activities of market hunters, gradually at first, and then rapidly, made serious inroads into these populations.

Massive US population today

North America can still boast enormous numbers of wild ducks, though. The total breeding population for 2005 was estimated to lie between

31 million and 32 million. The populations of some species make those of Britain and Ireland appear puny in the extreme. Take first of all the two main teal species of North America, blue-winged and green-winged. We have seen that population estimates for the former are in excess of 5,000,000. To these can be added nearly 3,000,000 green-winged teal. In Britain, we are told, the wintering teal population peaks at about 100,000 and there are a further 55,000 in Ireland. A quick calculation reveals that the combined teal population of our two islands is less than 2% of the North American one. A similar gulf exists between the numbers of wigeon on the two sides of the Atlantic. The 300,000 wintering here divide between Britain and Ireland roughly in the ratio of 2:1. Together they constitute a significant proportion of the northwest European population of 500,000. In mid-winter the population of the American wigeon is in the order of 2,500,000.

Paltry as our teal and wigeon numbers may appear in these comparisons, they can seem almost reasonable when we consider such species as pintail and shoveler. In autumn nearly 500,000 pintail move south across the United States. At roughly the same time 25,000 appear in Britain and a mere 2,000 in Ireland. For shoveler the situation is even worse. North America can claim a population of the order of 4,000,000. In mid-winter there are likely to be no more than 9,000 in Britain and 3,600 in Ireland.

Even that old reliable, the mallard, compares unfavourably with its American cousins. Throughout northwest Europe there are about 1,500,000 individuals. Of these there are an estimated 500,000 in Britain and a further 84,000 in Ireland. Across the Atlantic there are at least 9,000,000.

US and European counting methods

From some of the foregoing it is, I suspect, fairly obvious that I harbour a deep vein of cynicism when it comes to published figures for wildfowl. I must qualify this. I refer solely to figures published on this side of the Atlantic. I have considerably more faith in those for North America. In my estimation they do a great job in the States in assessing spring breeding numbers. The American Waterfowl Population Status Report is drawn up by using inputs from the Canadian Wildlife Service, U.S. Fish and Wildlife Service, state wildlife conservation agencies, provincial conservation agencies in Canada, Mexican wildlife authorities and many others, including hunters.

In Britain and Ireland the key term always used is 'estimates'. I think that guesstimates would be rather more appropriate. As a hunter, and I hope a responsible one, I want to know the size of quarry populations. I can then make an informed judgement about what is realistic in terms of taking a harvest. What I do not want to know, and what is all too often on offer, are population figures conjured up from counts at a number of (usually) accessible sites. Or, worse still, a patchwork put together on the basis of random counts and dubious second-hand information. And, not

Greylag goose – the winter migrants boost the smaller resident population in Britain and Ireland.

infrequently, figures provided by amateur twitchers who have little love for fieldsports. The simple reality is that figures are published, repeated at conferences, appear in what are supposed to be scientific papers and eventually become written in stone. Then, irrespective of their accuracy, they can be, and often are, used to make inroads into our sport. Doesn't happen? Don't you believe it. One of the greatest con jobs of all time was perpetrated on Irish goose shooters by just such methods. I will elaborate.

Following a massive decline of greylag numbers in Ireland in the 1960s (for reasons which are far from clear other than that they appear to have made a collective decision to relocate in Scotland) the Greenland whitefront was the only goose available to hunters. Then, in 1982, a four-year moratorium was imposed on the shooting of these birds on the basis that *published figures* clearly indicated a long-term decline. The catalyst for this con job was a 'scientific paper' published in 1979 which claimed that the world population of Greenland whitefronts had declined from 17,500-23,000 in the 1950s to 14,300-16,000 in the 1970s. Officialdom accepted these figures without question. Some years later I challenged them in a paper delivered to a conference on wild geese in Germany where I was one of a tiny handful of hunters present. I was then paid the supreme compliment by the conference organisers. They refused to publish my paper in the proceedings of the conference but, most generously, offered to condense it to a note. Needless to say, with the greatest politeness, I refused their offer.

It is the simplest thing in the world to demonstrate a decline in a population if you start with very high historical figures. Who can disprove them? This is exactly what happened in Ireland and was a pivotal point in my paper. Read on and judge for yourself. In Ireland there was virtually no goose counting in the 1950s – the decade from which, it was alleged, the decline had occurred. So how were the published figures obtained? Let me just give you a flavour of so-called 'science'.

1. A decline at Lough Gara in county Sligo from 500 in the 1950s was based upon 'locally acquired information'. Science at its very best!

2. A decline at Castleforbes in county Longford, again from 500 in
    the 1950s, was based upon a 'reliable source'.

Note the nice round starting figure of 500 in each case. Note also
'locally acquired information' and 'a reliable local source' – the author's
words, not mine. And remember this was written in the 1970s. Now let
us see what the same author thought about such information when writing
another 'scientific' paper about wild geese in 1958 ie the very period from
which he persuaded officialdom there has been a decline. I quote, 'local
information as to numbers is *totally unreliable*'. That same information cost
Irish goose shooters their only quarry. Twenty-four years later the 'four
year moratorium' is still in force. And, whenever the Greenland whitefront
is being discussed, that paper is still quoted with reverence. I made these
points in Germany but – surprise, surprise – no one wanted to hear them!

My cynicism in the matter of numbers as delivered by the birdy
fraternity had been well honed before the Greenland whitefront debacle.
It reached new heights when figures were published for wintering teal.
For a number of years in the 1980s and early 1990s I spent a considerable
amount of time, aided by hunters from all parts of Ireland, putting together
bag returns for the various quarry species. In the case of teal, with reasonable consistency from year to year, I found that the annual bag lay in the
range 40,000-50,000. A not unreasonable finding when it is noted that,

*Brent geese on parkland in a
Dublin suburb*

*Canada goose – a greatly valued quarry in
the USA*

45

on average, it amounts to less than half a teal per hunter over a five-month season. During those years the published figures for teal wintering in Ireland were all around 50,000. So, it would appear, we were removing in excess of 80% of the population each year. And yet, despite this inordinate take, the teal population to the present day remains as healthy as ever. Of course the birdy boys (and girls) had an explanation. Their figures could not possibly be wrong. The situation, they explained, was as follows: teal are continually moving through Ireland as winter progresses and on to the French coast and then on again as far as the Iberian peninsula. *All the time*, please note, and not just during periods of harsh weather! You can believe that if you like. All I can say is that there must be a mighty pile-up of teal in Portugal if this is the case.

There is a nice appendix to this teal story. British hunters must be far more efficient than Irish ones. Bag studies for Britain indicate an annual take of around 200,000 – quite realistic considering the relative numbers of hunters on the two islands. The problem is that the birdy boys claim that there are only 100,000 teal in Britain in mid-winter. Who was it said there are lies, damn lies and statistics?

I think that the answer to this particular conundrum is simple, but, unfortunately, it is not one that those who like to count wildfowl are prepared to countenance. There seems to be an assumption that a relatively small number of large concentrations of a particular species represent the overwhelming bulk of the wintering population. Following on from this if you count these big concentrations you have a pretty accurate indica-

The male pintail's call is a mellow whistle, whereas the female quacks, more like a mallard.

Greenland whitefront – subject of an assumed decline and consequent moratorium

tion of the total population. Unfortunately this is *not* the case and teal are a prime example. For every sizable pack, there are literally dozens and dozens of small groups and pairs that go unnoticed and unrecorded except by hunters. At this point I must be very blunt. In a long, and some might say misspent life, I have hunted teal over countless wetlands, big and small. Everywhere in fact from tiny streams and ponds to lakes, salt marshes and vast expanses of floodwater. On all those occasions I have never, ever, met someone counting wildfowl. Maybe it was too cold, too wet or too windy. And that is the experience of all my shooting acquaint-ances as well.

In debates of this nature I invariably return to my favourite bird, the red grouse. Despite my great affection for wildfowl and snipe, this bird is, for me, the ultimate challenge. Some months ago I was given a publi-cation of a bird-watching organisation. In it was the statement that, in Ireland, there has been a decline of over 66% in the species range between 1968/72 and 1988/91. An accompanying map showed, allegedly, where the bird is no longer found. Most extraordinary was the fact that some of these areas are ones in which I shoot grouse on a regular basis. I wrote to the organisation that produced the publication offering to make good the very many gaps in their knowledge. I also made the point that summer/ autumn surveys without using setting dogs were pointless. I got no reply.

Eventually I rang the organisation as I was afraid that their information (or more precisely lack of it) would be used by officialdom (as with the whitefront) to curtail grouse shooting.

I offered to take their representatives to places where they claim the grouse is absent and show them what is really there. They said they would get back to me. That was three months ago. Whether they do or do not, this is one bone I intend to hang on to. We lost the whitefront by default. We must not now lose the red grouse on the basis of misinformation. A final comment, and it is the same as that made concerning teal: in countless outings on the heather-covered uplands of Munster I have *never* met so much as one intrepid twitcher attempting to count grouse. Yet these 'experts' can rush into print and claim to be the ultimate authority on matters concerning the Irish red grouse.

CHAPTER FOUR

TIMES PAST

Centuries ago before those two ugly words 'reclamation' and 'drainage' entered the vocabulary of agriculture, Britain and Ireland provided wildfowl with some of the best habitat in the world. In additional to coastal wetlands, vast areas of low-lying land such as the Fens and the Shannon Basin must have, in winter, held ducks and geese in numbers of which latter-day hunters can only dream. Then there were the countless smaller wetlands. Some are now gone without trace; replaced by fields of lush green grass betraying nothing of what once was. Others, in some not too subtle way, provide hints as to their past before the hand of man descended. There may just be a rushy patch or two which, time and time again, successive farmers have tried to eradicate but have long since given up in this unequal struggle against Nature. Or there may be a weedy drainage trench under the hedgerow at the field's edge. Or there may be stubborn hollows in the best of pastures which can be relied upon to hold water, at least for a few days when autumn rains spill from the heavens.

For much of his history, mankind, despite all his ingenuity, did little to reduce those teeming wildfowl hordes. Ever alert and fleet of wing, the wild duck does not easily surrender itself. In earlier times few other than the falconer had the wherewithal to capture them. And his take was so tiny as to be insignificant. Whether falconry had its roots in sport or in the need to acquire food is a moot point. It is most likely that it was the former since, until the modern era, only the upper echelons of society were privileged to fly these noble birds and they of all people were hardly likely to be short of the proverbial crust.

Falconry appears to have reached Britain around 500 AD. It was without question the pre-eminent fieldsport for more than a millennium and only declined in popularity when reasonably efficient sporting guns began to appear in the 17th century. A variety of birds of prey have been used for falconry including eagles and owls, but the peregrine falcon has always held a special place in the sport. In speed of flight it is second-to-none and it has proven to be most amenable to training. In former eras a strict code existed in relation to the type of bird that a falconer was permitted to fly. Those at the top of the social pile flew peregrines, goshawks and certain exotic species. Clergymen formed the bottom tier of those allowed to participate in the sport and they were confined to flying the humble sparrow hawk. The merlin was ever the lady's bird. Whether this was because it was considered small and dainty like the fair sex or just another expression of chauvinism I do not know. I strongly suspect the latter.

As well as being used for the pursuit of wildfowl and game, the peregrine was employed to catch the grey heron, a bird much favoured for banquets during the Middle Ages.

Sometime, probably in the early Middle Ages, mankind began to seriously exploit the one real chink in the wild duck's armour...its flight-less period during eclipse. On broad, deep waters they were probably relatively safe but there were countless other wetlands that lent themselves to the equivalent of a duck round-up. A wide net, often many hundreds of yards in length, was set up in something approaching a semi-circle. At the centre of this semi-circle was a netted funnel into which ducks were driven. Depending upon location, the drive was conducted using a fleet of small boats or by shouting humanity splashing through a marsh. Mallard were the main species taken in this manner and there are reports of thousands being caught in a single round-up. The practice was finally outlawed in Britain in 1710 when it had become apparent that in some parts, wild duck populations were dwindling. Drainage works were also beginning to have a negative effect on numbers during this period. The round-ups were especially serious because countless young birds, the future breeding stock, were being taken.

In passing, it is worthy of note that the young of several species other than wildfowl were also highly-regarded fare. Young wood pigeons, or squabs as they were commonly called, were considered a particular delicacy. As they grew on the flimsy nest, a piece of netting was tied loosely over them to prevent their escape. The mesh was of sufficient size to allow the parents to continue to feed them. In coastal communities in both Britain and Ireland the young of certain sea birds such as gannets were collected and salted for later consumption. Their capture could be a hazardous business as it sometimes involved being lowered down a cliff-face on a rope. On occasions the catcher used a wire noose attached to a pole to whip his prey off a ledge.

Unlike their resident cousins, migratory wildfowl remained relatively free from human attention until two very different events deprived them of an age-old immunity. One of these events was the development of the sporting gun. Of this more later.

The 17th century decoy trap

The other was the invention of the duck decoy. Not the model duck for which we are indebted to the native Americans but a permanent, partly-netted water body first developed in Holland. In fact the word decoy is derived from the Dutch word 'eendekoi', literally, a duck cage. At first known as 'duckcoy', this eventually became 'decoy'. Later the word 'decoy' developed the more general meaning of attracting or luring.

Many great inventions have had their origins in a moment of inspiration. Sometimes the simple observation of an everyday occurrence was the catalyst that prompted an idea. The cats' eyes that adorn our roads are a case in point. Some inspired and lucky individual realised the potential for road safety by mimicking the glistening eyes of a creature of the night. That same lucky individual patented his idea and was swiftly propelled to a life of financial security. In the case of the duck decoy the idea was spawned, in all probability, when someone noticed how wildfowl respond (from the safety of water) to a predator on the bank.

Anyone familiar with the countryside will be aware of the various responses of its avian inhabitants when a predator or perceived predator appears on the scene. In some cases these responses are essentially vocal, such as the excited chattering of magpies when a fox crosses their patch or the high-pitched calls of blackbirds and wrens when a sparrow hawk drifts into view. In other cases the response takes the form of that extraordinary spectacle of mobbing. Birds of prey in particular are subjected to these mock attacks which, at first sight, seem to verge on the seriously inadvisable. But the perpetrators of these attacks seem to know exactly what they are doing, as the objects of their torment never seem to turn on them. I remember once, on a glorious sunny August day on the Isle of Skye, watching a golden eagle soaring majestically above the heather. Literally out of the blue a pair of rooks appeared and proceeded to dive bomb it and subject it to every manner of aerial attack. I was certain

The tapering shape of a classic duck decoy pipe showing, in the foreground, the small trapping end in which the ducks were caught

The kooikerhondje – a dog bred specially for decoy work

sure that those rooks would come to a sticky end as the price of their temerity. But I need not have worried. The eagle merely flapped away without so much as a backward glance at its oppressors. I would like to think that small birds that engage in mobbing pick up some sort of cue that the predator is well-fed and is thus happy to vacate the area for a quiet life. But maybe I am guilty of a touch of anthropomorphism. If so, *mea culpa*, because anthropomorphism is very much the nectar upon which the 'antis' flourish. No true hunter, and I number myself as such, would ever engage in such delusions.

In relation to mobbing I have always had more than a little sympathy for the grey heron. It seems to be an automatic target for every passing rook and jackdaw. Herons have been known to take small ducklings but I cannot conceive that they represent any manner of threat to corvids, be they young or old.

Many species of wildfowl mob by following on water, at a discreet distance, a predator on *terra firma*, in particular a fox. They will often follow it along a river bank for quite a long way, keeping at all times that respectable distance. In a moment of inspiration someone obviously

Part of the curved shape of a decoy pipe showing the netting supported by hoops and side views of the screens (right).

realised that this predator response could be put to good use to capture ducks. Essentially they could be lured into some sort of catching device by using a suitable predator substitute such as a dog. And so was born the duck decoy. First constructed in the 16th century, their use quickly spread from Holland to many European countries. By the 1650s a number were operational in England, particularly the east, but strangely there is no record of a duck decoy in Scotland. Best documented is the one constructed in St James's Park in London in 1665 for King Charles II.

The basic layout of a decoy is a central lake, ideally between one and three acres, from which radiate out a number of curving channels called pipes. They were usually located in places where there were no other nearby lakes as this ensured a good concentration of ducks. Some were developed from an existing small lake but the majority were specially dug out by hand, a laborious business when one considers that in addition to the central area, two or more pipes extended away for up to seventy yards. Trees and shrubs were set all around the decoy so that the ducks would not be subjected to disturbance. Some decoys were constructed to supply the local 'big house' and the surplus catch went to market. Others were specifically designed as commercial ventures.

In operating the decoy the basic principle was to lure the ducks from the central pond body into one of the pipes. The pipes were covered with netting which was supported by semi-circular hoops set quite close together. The first hoop, lying at the mouth of the pipe, was very large, some twenty feet in width and fifteen feet in height.

In the early decoys the hoops were made of wood, mainly elm and willow. Later they were made of iron. Passing along the pipe, the hoops grew progressively smaller until at the furthest extremity they measured little more than two feet in width and two feet in height. The pipes were curved so that the ducks would not realise that they were being drawn into an ever-diminishing space. At the narrow termination of the pipe was a small, roughly square wooden frame to which a net could be attached. The net was not dissimilar to the keep net used by coarse anglers to retain their catch. It had its own supportive hoops so that it could stand erect. One of these nets could accommodate thirty ducks, sometimes more. The wooden frame to which it was attached was grooved so that a board could be dropped to secure the ducks once they were in the net. This final catching point was purposely located in a bright, open spot so that the ducks would develop a false sense of security through seeing the sky above them.

Like all birds, ducks take off into the wind. This was the reason for having a number of pipes in the decoy. At a certain point along the pipe the ducks would be flushed, so it was imperative that a head wind was always available.

In operating a decoy it was necessary to attract wild birds to the central pond and from there to the correct pipe for that particular day. Some decoy traps relied upon tame ducks to lure in the wild ones. Others were fed on the banks and in the shallows at the mouth of the pipe. In some cases a combination of call ducks and feeding was used. Dabbling ducks were the almost exclusive targets of the decoy men, and mallard and teal usually constituted the bulk of the catch. Smaller numbers of shoveler, wigeon and pintail were also taken. Diving ducks rarely figured in the catch. There were two reasons for this. They cannot be attracted as readily as their dabbling relations by feeding. Also, because of their considerable skills of diving and swimming underwater, the few that did get lured into a pipe tended to escape the clutches of the decoy man. It was not uncommon for a decoy to yield 3,000 ducks in a season, and a few caught double this number.

For a decoy to work, one further structure must now be described. Along one bank of each pipe ran a series of staggered screens behind which the decoy man could conceal himself and issue instructions to his dog. These screens were composed of a wooden frame into which reeds were woven. The decoy man could make a temporary small slit in the

Staggered reed-covered screens which were used to conceal the decoy man and from behind which the dog would suddenly appear on command.

reeds to view the ducks. The screens were at least six feet in height and at least twice this length. From the water side, they gave the appearance of a continuous wall. When there were enough ducks on the water at the entrance to the pipe, the decoy man would order his dog to appear outside the screen, run along the bank and pass out of sight behind the second screen. Obeying the predator response of their kind, the ducks would swim into the pipe in order to follow this malignant creature. The dog would then be ordered to carry out a similar manoeuvre further along the pipe. Then, finally, when the decoy man was happy that the ducks had been lured sufficiently along the pipe, he would show himself, causing them to rise in panic and fly down the pipe to their doom. In Holland a red and white dog, not dissimilar to a fox, was specially bred. It was called the kooikerhondje and the breed exists to the present day.

Duck decoys were in active use for well over two centuries and were important as sources of fresh meat during the winter months. However, they gradually went into decline as the 19th century progressed. There were a number of reasons for their demise. Wildfowl habitat and thus wildfowl numbers were declining as more and more drainage schemes were undertaken, Additionally, disturbance as a result of shooting was becoming a major problem. A decoy could only yield a constant harvest if it were free from all disturbance. Towards the end of the 19th century Sir Ralph Payne-Gallwey attempted to census the decoys present in Britain and Ireland. Whilst his survey was almost certainly incomplete, he was able to locate 188 in England, 22 in Ireland and only 5 in Wales. Of these, only 44 were still operational when he published his findings in 1886. By 1910 there were only 3 left in Ireland.

Working decoys have now all but passed into history. At the end of the 20th century there were only 4 left in Britain and none at all in Wales or Ireland. In Ireland I can only find two place names which bear witness to their former existence. One of these lies just a few miles from Clonmel in County Tipperary. The Decoy Bog, as it is known, was a marshy, wooded area extending to some 70 acres. It was drained a few years ago and now betrays little of its former role. The other, known simply as Decoy, is located at Dunlavin near Blessington in County Wicklow. It covers almost 200 acres.

The former large decoy trap at Mallow, Ireland (1910) which was one of only three in the country at that time.

The four working decoys remaining in England are at Borough Fen near Peterborough, Slimbridge, Boarstall in Buckinghamshire and Abbotsbury in Dorset. Ducks caught in these decoys are no longer destined for the table. Instead they are ringed and released. Large numbers of teal in particular have been caught and ringed at decoys over the last few decades.

Boarstall Decoy, which now belongs to the National Trust, is a place of great solitude and beauty and is well worth a visit. Set in the middle of broad open fields it is surrounded by 15 acres of woodlands which were originally planted to ensure that the decoy itself would be free of all disturbance. Oak, ash and hazels abound in the woodland. The decoy was constructed between 1691 and 1697 to supply Boarstall Tower. Presently there are three pipes emanating from the central three-acre lake but there may have been more originally. One can certainly make out the line of what was a probable fourth. The place is also a mini nature reserve and hosts a surprising range of creatures. As soon as we entered the wood a green woodpecker flew up into the trees complaining noisily at the intrusion. Shortly afterwards a muntjac bounded across the path in front of us.

Considering the teeming masses of ducks that move south across the North American continent each autumn it is extraordinary that, with a tiny number of exceptions, decoys were not constructed there. One might have expected that the rapidly expanding population would have provided a ready market for their produce. People from every country in Europe crossed to the New World so that there can be little doubt that knowledge of decoy construction and use went with them. It can only be assumed that powder and shot were cheap and readily available. Certainly enormous numbers of wildfowl reached the markets every winter. There is of course the point that pioneer peoples were, more than most, conversant with guns. Indeed, in the early settlements in many far-flung corners of the earth, one's very survival depended on one's proficiency with them.

It is worth visiting Boarstall, an elaborate decoy lake and trap which was completed in 1697.

But even allowing for this, the absence of decoys is surprising because the decoy-caught bird, being free of lead shot and its resultant damage, represented a superior product for the discerning eater. In relation to the sale of shot birds it is interesting to note that the practice ceased in North America in 1918. By way of contrast, with the exception of gadwall and goldeneye, it is quite legitimate to sell wild ducks both in Britain and Ireland.

In relation to decoys, the best documented one in North America was of comparatively recent construction. Inspired by the late Sir Peter Scott it was constructed at the Delta Waterfowl Research Centre in Manitoba in 1940. Its purpose was solely to catch ducks for ringing. Sadly it appears that it is no longer in use.

Development of firearms

The development of efficient firearms radically improved mankind's capacity to harvest wildfowl, whether for food or for sport. It is generally agreed that the gun appeared on the English scene in the early years of the 14th century. As a weapon of war its use was becoming increasingly common during this period. Whilst there is little documentary evidence of the gun's first use in the hunting field, it is reasonable to assume that it was not too long delayed. Initially, though, its impact on wildfowl populations must have been strictly limited. The powder charge had to be ignited manually, an operation clearly ill-suited to the downing of fast-moving quarry. Presumably in those early days, the only chance was to place a large charge of shot into a company of ducks from a place of concealment.

With the passage of time, human ingenuity gradually refined the workings of the gun. A number of well-defined advances shared a common theme. Essentially a mechanism was incorporated that ignited the powder. First, around 1450, the matchlock appeared. This had a slow-burning fuse or match which was brought into contact with the powder when the trigger was pulled. Whilst clearly an advance on manual ignition, the matchlock's use in the hunting field must also have been limited. Imagine the difficulty of stalking a bird or lying in wait trying to keep the match alight. All the hazards of mist, wind and rain would have conspired against it. Then, some sixty years later, the first of the firelock guns was invented. These had a mechanism which generated sparks that ignited a priming charge which, in turn, set off the main charge.

The wheel-lock

The wheel-lock was the first of the firelocks. When the trigger was pulled it caused a rough-edged steel wheel to revolve against a piece of iron pyrites. This substance is a hard, sulphur-containing ore of iron sometimes called fools' gold because of the similarity in colour to the precious metal. The abrasive contact generated a shower of sparks. This capacity of pyrites to produce sparks when struck had been known since ancient times; indeed the word pyrites is derived from the Ancient Greek word pyr meaning fire. With the advent of the wheel-lock the hunter now had a reasonable chance of bringing down a moving target. There was very little time lag between the trigger being pulled and the explosion of the main powder charge.

The flint-lock

About a hundred years later in the early 1600s the wheel-lock gave way to a new and more efficient firelock called the flintlock. Its mechanism was based upon a spring action which caused a steel striker to hit against a piece of flint so again generating a flurry of sparks. Flint is a form of quartz. The sparks it generated ignited gunpowder in an adjacent priming pan. With increasing refinement the flintlock remained the standard firing action for the next 200 years. In the right hands it was to become a formidable weapon for the pursuit of wildfowl. The redoubtable Colonel Peter Hawker who lived from 1786 to 1853 and who published the shooting classic *Instructions to Young Sportsmen in all that relates to Guns and Shooting* shot several thousand ducks and geese with a flintlock in the course of a lifetime devoted to hunting game of all species.

The percussion-lock

The discovery of a chemical compound called mercuric fulminate in 1779 marked the beginning of the final chapter in the history of firing mechanisms. When this substance is struck it detonates. The significance of this fact was not lost on gunsmiths who quickly saw the potential of a percussion-based firing system. The era of the firelocks was finally ending and by the middle of the 19th century the percussion lock had become a standard feature of sporting guns. When, later in the century, the cartridge was developed, the mercuric fulminate was incorporated into a percussion cap. Then, in the 1930s, mercuric fulminate also began to pass into history. It was replaced by cheaper and more reliable compounds that could be detonated by percussion.

The cartridge

The development of the cartridge finally did away with the tedious business of ramming powder and shot down the barrel, a minimal problem, perhaps, for the early punt gunners who could hope for at least a reasonable return for the discharge of a single shot, but for other hunters of that era, the reloading process clearly imposed restrictions on their sport. Imagine those golden moments at evening flight when a bird is down and yet another pack is engaging in a final circuit. You and I are liable

The modern cartridge has made re-loading infinitely quicker and more convenient – it is hard to imagine how the adrenaline-fueled shooter coped in the days of the cumbersome firelock.

to fumble with cartridges in the adrenaline-inspired excitement of the moment. Our counterparts of long ago must have undergone a thousand agonies as they attempted to get powder and shot into place in time for a shot. Some though, it would seem, became highly proficient at the task and were able to make bags that would more than satisfy a hunter of the present day.

By the late 1860s the breech loading shotgun and the modern cartridge with its central percussion cap were being widely used. After this, little has changed other than the development of more sophisticated propellant powders.

The hunter now had at his disposal a weapon that could be fired and reloaded quickly and which could throw consistent shot patterns. For the (mainly) wealthy minority who could afford to spend their winters in search of ducks and geese, these must have been magnificent times. Wildfowl were still extraordinarily abundant and there were virtually no restrictions on the sport. A range of different bores or gauges were manufactured including some mighty shoulder guns capable of throwing several ounces of lead at high flying birds.

The description of a shotgun by the size of its bore was, and still is, curious in the extreme. It refers to the number of spherical balls of lead whose diameter is the same as that of the barrel and which collectively weigh one pound. Thus in the case of the twelve bore: twelve such balls of lead weigh a pound. It has always been something of a mystery to me why shotguns were not classified like rifles on the basis of bore diameter. The variations due to different degrees of choke would be of little significance. Four bores, eight bores and ten bores were manufactured, mainly for coastal use. Some of these, not surprisingly, were very heavy guns and demanded that the hunter be a man of no mean physique. Nowadays they have been largely abandoned in favour of the magnum 12 bore. It weighs little more than a standard game gun but, being chambered for a three inch cartridge, can fire a shot charge equivalent to that of a 10 bore.

Punt gunning by both professionals and sporting amateurs gained considerable popularity in the later decades of the 19th century. We will meet these mighty men and their mighty guns in a later chapter.

CHAPTER FIVE

POPULATIONS, HUNTING AND MORTALITY

Hunters of previous generations are unlikely to have given much thought to the effects of their activities on the populations of quarry species. By and large they did not have to anyway. Wildfowl of all species abounded, suitable habitat was effectively unlimited and the hunters themselves were not exactly equipped with weapons of mass destruction. In addition, in both Britain and Ireland, the numbers of people entitled to engage in the sport were very limited.

But much was to change. Several factors began to combine to cause serious reductions in wildfowl populations. Reference has already been made to the steady erosion of wetland habitats by drainage works. To this must be added the development of ever more efficient firearms and an enormous rise in the levels of commercial hunting. Mention has been made of the massacre of American wood duck and eider. And such declines at the hands of commercial hunters were not confined to wildfowl. The sad history of the over-exploitation of the bison has been well documented.

By the beginning of the 20th century the North American passenger pigeon, the most multitudinous land bird ever to grace the Earth, was passing into extinction.

Eventually the message got through. Wild populations cannot forever absorb the losses occasioned by commercial hunting. As we have seen, wisdom prevailed in North America and in 1918 legislation was introduced outlawing the practice. But over fifty years were to pass before the enactment of similar legislation in Britain. And in Britain the ban on the sale of shot wildfowl was confined to geese. It was not too long before the positive effects of this became apparent. Especially in Scotland, pinkfoot and greylag numbers began to increase. In relation to wild ducks the fact that it is still legitimate to sell them is of little consequence. Modern man (and his better half) have grown lazy and it is an increasingly rare person who can be bothered with the hassle of preparing birds for the table. On occasions I offer my surplus birds to friends and neighbours and a not uncommon response is, 'Will you pluck them for me?' It is my understanding that some of the commercial pheasant shoots often experience difficulty when it comes to disposing of the bag, which is a tragedy because there is no finer protein source than the flesh of fowl.

For hunters and game managers of the 21st century it is vital to have a good knowledge of wild populations and an understanding of the factors which impinge on them. They must be in a position to ensure that the annual take does not exceed the available surplus, always assuming that in a given year there is in fact a surplus.

Before considering the effects of hunting on wild populations, it is first necessary to look at the various factors that influence population trends. Every population usually experiences an annual recruitment and

Population gains and losses

suffers an annual loss. I say usually because, for some species, there can be years in which there is a total or near-total breeding failure. The pale bellied Brent goose which breeds in Arctic Canada and winters in Ireland is a case in point. In Britain the imported red-legged partridge can suffer a similar fate in a wet summer. Recruitment relies upon the addition of the year's young and upon immigration. Losses result from mortality and emigration.

In an environment untouched by the hand of man, and there are admittedly precious few of these left in these islands, wild populations will tend to fluctuate around a mean according to the relative levels of recruitment and loss. Once mankind enters the equation, however, matters become rather more complicated, especially if he decides to exploit a population. Should he also accidentally or purposefully degrade the environment by some activity, a reduced holding-capacity is the almost inevitable outcome. We saw for example significant losses in wetland habitats following accession to the then-European Economic Community. Generous reclamation grants were made available to farmers which resulted in the loss of countless ponds and other small but vitally important wet places. The minds of politicians are frequently hard to comprehend. But fortunately we have now entered an era in which they have decided we must produce less food and, in consequence, landowners are now being rewarded for preserving natural habitats. Long may this last.

In relation to recruitment, much centres around weather conditions during the breeding season. In an earlier chapter mention was made of the importance of insect life for young ducklings. Cool, wet springs yield fewer insects and this, together with the increased likelihood of chilling can have a catastrophic effect on broods and thus recruitment levels.

Three main factors are responsible for mortalities in wild populations. They are starvation, disease and predation. It is most likely that, in any one case, death results from a combination of these factors. A bird on an impoverished diet is much more likely to fall victim to parasites or predators than its well-fed colleague. It is not generally realised just how short many lifespans are in the wilds. Take for example the mallard. From the day that it emerges from the egg, its life expectancy, on average, is no more than 1.2 years. And this is in regions where there is no hunting.

A mallard entering eclipse, skulking in vegetation.

The woodcock fares a little better with an average life expectancy of 2.2 years.

Populations are at their greatest in late summer and early autumn at the conclusion of the breeding season. At this time of year, food supplies are still abundant so there is little competition. But then, as autumn gives way to winter, these supplies dwindle and competition for what is left grows more and more intense. Natural Selection soon begins to exact its annual toll.

Whilst populations remain high, predators and parasites are provided with their best opportunities. The more numerous the members of a prey species, the easier it is for predators to go about their business. Equally, the parasites responsible for disease have more opportunities to spread to new hosts. A direct analogy can be drawn to the spread of infectious diseases in humans. One is far more likely to catch a cold or 'flu in a school or workplace where people congregate than it is in the relative isolation of one's own home. Parasites have evolved all sorts of strategies to ensure that their offspring reach new hosts. Some rely upon simple bodily contact.

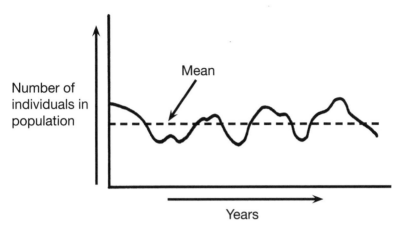

Fluctuations in the numbers of individuals in a wild population over a long number of years.

Others, in particular viruses, may rely upon droplet transmission. In this case the agents of infection leave the body of an infected individual in tiny water droplets in exhaled air. If there are potential new hosts in the immediate vicinity there is every chance that they will be taken in during inhalation. Yet others rely upon blood-sucking insects to pass from host to host. The rabbit flea, for example, transmits the Myxoma virus which is responsible for myxomatosis. The female Anopheline mosquito carries plasmodium, the organism responsible for malaria.

In passing, it is appropriate to make mention of avian 'flu. This disease is caused by a large group of viruses but only a few of them are capable of killing birds. There has been much concern amongst duck hunters on account of the fact that the Asian strain H5N1 has been responsible for a number of human deaths. Presently human beings can only be infected by contact with an infected bird. The fear is that the virus will mutate into a form which will have the capacity to pass from human to human. The likelihood of this happening, however, now appears to be diminishing.

Migratory bird populations, and these include many of our important wintering wildfowl, can, in addition to the causes of mortality mentioned, suffer severe losses during the actual migratory flight. The sheer effort of flying many hundreds or thousands of miles takes an inevitable toll. Adverse weather conditions are a constant threat. Then there are the dangers, especially for disorientated young birds, attendant upon touching down en route in unfamiliar and threatening places. During periods of stormy weather it is not unusual for fishermen operating on the North Sea to find woodcock floating on the water. These are birds passing to and fro between breeding grounds in Scandinavia and the Baltic States and wintering grounds in Britain and Ireland.

Because of the potential for loss during migration it makes very good sense to ensure that wildfowl leave the wintering grounds in the best possible condition. Essentially this means giving them a good period for undisturbed feeding prior to departure. I would venture to suggest that this period should be a minimum of one month after the cessation of shooting. They should then be able to lay down sufficient fatty and other reserves to sustain them on their journey and also set them up for the forthcoming breeding season.

For wildfowl, the maintenance of quality habitat and where it is possible, the creation of new habitat, must be the key to the future. This has long been recognised in North America where funds collected from the sale of Habitat Conservation Stamps are used for these purposes. In Canada alone over 30,000,000 dollars have been raised since 1985. We are at a stage when most wildfowl populations can only expand to a significant degree if the environment is so engineered as to have an increased capacity to meet their needs. At present most wild duck and goose populations in Britain are stable or increasing slightly. This would tend to confirm the

Canada geese – an introduced species whose population in Britain expanded dramatically following the flooding of worked-out gravel pits.

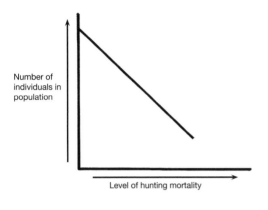

Additive mortality.

belief that the environment has little spare 'holding capacity'. The most notable exception is the pinkfoot which has shown a dramatic increase in numbers since the last decades of the 20th century. This in part, as we have seen, was due to the banning of commercial hunting. But there is more to it than that. It is my belief that, particularly in Scotland, extra quality habitat in the form of an expansion in the acreage of spring and autumn cereal crops played an important part.

Another example of the benefits of habitat creation is to be found in the case of the introduced Canada goose. When, in the post-war years in southeast England, motorway construction and other building projects created an insatiable demand for gravel, countless pits, some extending over many acres, were dug out. When finally exhausted of gravel, many of them were flooded and adapted to the needs of wildfowl. Within a few years the Canada goose population began to expand. Tufted duck also benefited substantially from these developments.

So far we have considered the major factors that govern the destinies of wild populations. In particular we have looked at the main causes of natural mortality. If mortality due to hunting is now brought into the equation, a new vista opens. It would seem logical in theory that if mankind removes

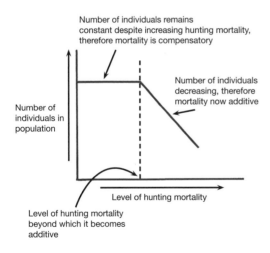

Compensatory mortality.

a segment of a population then that population should decline as hunting mortality combines with natural mortality. For some species this is indeed the case, as hunting mortality does increase the overall mortality. Ecologists, unsurprisingly, refer here to additive mortality. Strangely, however, mortality due to hunting is not additive for all species. Research has shown that there are species from which it is possible to take an annual harvest without detriment to their long-term viability. The only explanation for this is that there is now a reduced level of natural mortality. Ecologists refer here to compensatory mortality ie nature has a form of built-in compensation in which deaths due to hunting replace (to a degree) rather than add to, deaths from natural causes. For the hunter two questions immediately arise. Why is it that compensatory mortality is a reality for some species but not for others? And, for those species which exhibit a level of compensatory mortality, just what is that level? In relation to this second question a point must clearly be reached at which hunting mortalities are so great that they become additive.

First let us try to find an explanation for compensatory mortality. To do this we must return to the three main causes of natural mortality: starvation, disease and predation.

During and immediately after the breeding season food supplies are generally near to a maximum. Plants, which are the first stage of the food chain, usually have ideal conditions during the summer months to manufacture food in the process of photosynthesis. Some duck species feed directly on plants, others rely upon the animal life supported by the plants. Either way there is for a while plenty of food which means that competition levels are low. But this happy state of affairs will not last for long. As temperatures begin to decline, the capacity of plants to produce food diminishes and the serious business of competition for what is available grows daily more intense. Simply put, there is not enough food to go round so that the weak must starve or, reduced to some emaciated state, fall victim to predators or parasites. But if hunting takes place, the resulting cull means that there are fewer individuals competing and there are thus less deaths from starvation or starvation-related causes. If, as is the case with mallard, the greater part of the bag is taken early in the season, so much the better. Numbers have been reduced before the period of most severe food shortage arrives. But should hunters take a heavy toll late in the season, the decline in food sources is likely to have already impacted on the population. Reflect upon the implications of this latter scenario.

In the case of predators and parasites the story is similar. As the early autumn population decreases in the face of hunting pressures, both groups of organisms find it increasingly hard to ply their respective trades. With less prey at their disposal, predators will have to expend more energy in order to feed themselves. Some will not survive, others will, at least in part, turn their attentions to other prey species. The net result is that there will be a decline in deaths due to predation. For parasites, a reduced number of hosts means that they experience greater difficulty in transmitting to new hosts. Fewer infections means fewer deaths and thus, once again, a reduction in the level of natural mortality.

Our knowledge of the factors that cause hunting mortality to be additive for some species and compensatory for others is still far from complete. In relation to wildfowl we can generalise to a certain extent. For most species of geese, hunting mortality is additive but for most species of duck, it is compensatory. So where do we start? We know that species which display some degree of compensatory mortality have certain well-defined characteristics. In particular, they have a high reproductive rate. As well as this, the young tend to reach maturity quickly and individuals generally live short lives.

Effects of hunting on grouse populations

Away from the world of wildfowl the best example of a species which shows a high degree of compensatory mortality is the red grouse. Because of the economic importance of this bird to many of the more remote parts of northern England and Scotland, it has been the subject of extensive studies. Grouse usually lay eight or nine eggs, sometimes more, and it is quite common for a large proportion of the chicks to reach maturity. They grow exceptionally quickly. Young grouse take to the wing when they are only thirteen or fourteen days old. They are short-lived birds with few surviving beyond their second year. In a nutshell, grouse display all the features that we associate with a species for which hunting mortality is compensatory. Studies have shown that it is possible to shoot as much as

60% of the late summer population, possibly even 65%, without detriment to the population. There cannot, realistically, be a better example than this in the world of hunted birds.

Effects of hunting on mallard populations

If pride of place in the matter of compensatory mortality must be awarded to the red grouse, the mallard is not too far behind. No species of wildfowl has been the subject of more studies, so we know a great deal about it. There is though one complicating factor. Many hundreds of thousands are released for shooting each year. Because of this there is considerable difficulty in ascertaining trends in truly wild populations. With this caveat in mind there is little doubt that mallard do meet the typical profile of a species suited to compensatory mortality. Clutches are large, ten to twelve eggs most commonly, ducklings grow and mature quickly and, as noted in a previous chapter, the life expectancy on hatching is a mere 1.2 years. Conventional wisdom has it that it is possible to harvest somewhere approaching 50% of the late summer population. An added advantage is that the mallard is an early breeder so that, should the first clutch be lost, there is still plenty of time for a replacement one. The precise size of the annual wild mallard bag in Britain is not known. However, there is a widely-held view that it is not far short of the critical 50%. Much the same probably holds true for Ireland. If this is the case, any significant increase in the annual harvest could have serious repercussions for the species. In North America it is thought that the percentage take is somewhat lower, possibly not reaching 40% of the late summer population.

Much less is known about the effects of hunting on the other major dabbling duck species. Since their biology is basically similar to the mallard's, it is not unreasonable to suppose that birds such as wigeon and teal enjoy fairly similar levels of compensatory mortality. Like mallard they produce fairly large clutches and the young mature equally quickly. It is worth remembering however that they are largely migratory, a fact that is likely to sustain higher levels of natural mortality than is the case with species which are largely sedentary.

Diving ducks do not appear to have attracted the level of scientific study afforded their dabbling cousins. However, as their biology is not too different to that of dabblers, one might expect that matters relating to mortality would be broadly similar: in fact this is not the case. It is recommended that the maximum harvest should not exceed 20% of the late summer population although I can personally find little logic in this. Whilst, admittedly, I have never come across 12 plus broods of tufted ducks or pochard, something which is not uncommon with mallard, I have seen plenty of broods of 6 or 7 healthy ducklings. It may possibly be that because they breed rather later, sometimes not until June in the case of tufted ducks, they are less likely to replace a lost clutch. To what extent this might impact on the late summer population I simply do not know.

Effects of hunting on wild geese populations

Turning now to the wild geese we have noted that conventional wisdom has it that for most species hunting mortality is additive. We have also noted the apparent anomaly in this respect that two species in these islands, the pinkfoot and the Canada goose, are enjoying expansions despite (especially in the case of the pinkfoot) serious hunting pressures. It is also worthy of note that across the Atlantic numbers of snow geese are also on the up. The present healthy state of its population is such that states like New York and Virginia are allowing a daily bag limit of 15. In Canada the limit is even higher. The provinces of Quebec, Manitoba, Alberta and Saskatchewan all allow 20.

Against this background we must address two issues. First, why is hunting mortality additive for most wild goose species? The answer, it would seem, is because their life profiles contain none of those characteristics of wild ducks which promote some degree of compensatory mortality. In particular, geese lay fewer eggs. Normal clutch sizes are in the range of 3–7. And whereas most ducks start to breed (and thus contribute to the population) when they are a year old, most geese do not do so until their third or fourth year. There is also some evidence, especially in the case of the Greenland whitefront, that there are segments of the population (other than the young) which do not breed. It may also be remembered that compensatory mortality is associated with birds that lead relatively short lives. Many wild geese, on the other hand, live to a ripe old age.

As to the anomaly of the two goose species which are doing well despite heavy shooting, it seems clear that they are the beneficiaries of the increased amount of good quality habitat that has become available. If, as is likely, this is the case, it is reasonable to suppose that the increases will continue until the holding capacity of the environment has been reached. Only at this juncture will it be possible to make a judgement as to whether hunting mortality is indeed additive in geese such as the pinkfoot.

Effects of predators

Returning again to compensatory mortality there is, from the hunter's perspective, one major downside. Game/wildfowl conservation requires, inter alia, the control of predators. Unfortunately the principle underlying compensatory mortality applies just as much to the populations of many predatory species as it does to their prey. But this area of biology has received less attention. The implications are disheartening. Continuous and whole-hearted predator control may well be necessary to make a difference. There would seem to be little point in low-intensity predator control if the numbers removed are simply balanced by a reduced level of natural mortality. This is especially the case in Ireland where the part-time nature of gamekeeping means that predator control tends to be spasmodic and is rarely conducted at high intensity.

CHAPTER SIX

LEAD SHOT, NON-TOXIC SHOT AND CRIPPLING LOSSES

Realisation of a problem associated with the use of lead shot against wildfowl can be traced back to 1884. In that year, George Bird Grinnell reported that at two lakes in Texas – Stephenson Lake at Galveston and Lake Surprise some 25 miles away to the northeast – ducks, geese and swans were frequently found dead, sick or unable to fly. Similar occurrences were noted at Curritock Sound on the North Carolina coast. These birds showed no external signs of injury and they were said locally to be suffering from 'croup'.

On investigation it was found that the gizzards of affected birds contained particles of lead mixed with the usual content of sand and small stones. Some of the lead particles were so small that they equated to number 12 shot. Some 65 years later, F. C. Bellrose published an important paper highlighting lead poisoning as a mortality factor in wildfowl populations.

Some background is necessary to understand the significance of these findings. Before the enzymes of the gut can effectively attack ingested food, it must be crushed to provide a large surface area for this attack. Mammals have specially designed back teeth, premolars and molars, to achieve this objective. Birds, in contrast, use their gizzards. These are muscular organs with a tough lining in which small particles of grit are held to assist in grinding down the food. Anyone who has ever prepared a turkey's gizzard for the Christmas feast will be familiar with the hard, convoluted lining. The problem begins when wildfowl pick up spent shot. It passes along the gut to the gizzard where the lead, as a result of the crushing activity and the action of digestive juices, is converted into soluble compounds which enter the bird's blood. These toxic compounds of lead are transported around the body causing all sorts of damage. A range of organs, in particular the liver and kidneys, are at risk and death is likely to occur.

Spent lead-shot ingested

Lead is a soft metal with a high density (11.3 g/cm^3). These qualities make it an ideal material for ballistic purposes. When lead pellets strike a bird they can cause a quick kill by severing a major blood vessel/nerve or by the shock of impact as the metal flattens against hard tissues. In the vast majority of cases only a tiny number of pellets actually find the target. The rest, typically a few hundred, are dispersed into the environment where those that fall into water may well be ingested by wildfowl. Bellrose, and later many others, recorded a considerable number of die-offs in America as a result of the uptake of spent lead shot. For wildfowl hunters, the writing was clearly on the wall. In Europe far fewer die-offs were recorded but the same ominous threat was all to real. For example, J. O'Halloran and colleagues found that twenty mute swans died in the vicinity of Lough Neagh in Northern Ireland as a result of ingesting pellets from a nearby clay pigeon shooting ground.

In the 1970s lead shot used by anglers to sink their bait came under scrutiny in Britain. This was triggered by recognition of a serious decline in the number of mute swans on the Thames and other rivers. Exceptionally high levels of lead were found in the blood of dead swans and eventually in 1987 legislation outlawing the use of lead weights for angling came into effect.

There has been some debate as to whether ducks accidentally ingest lead pellets as grit or purposefully select them in mistake for the seeds of aquatic plants. The balance of evidence would appear to support the latter contention. In my experience, I have examined many hundreds of ducks' gizzards: those of pochard tend to contain more pellets than those of other species. Seeds are a favoured food of pochard. In the case of mallard, which are probably the least conservative of ducks when it comes to the matter of diet, I examined gizzards sent to me by hunters from many parts of Ireland. Less than 3% of these gizzards were contaminated and over half of these contained only a single pellet.

Once the problem of lead poisoning became apparent, a considerable amount of experimentation took place in an attempt to assess the magnitude of the problem posed by spent shot in the environment. In the main this experimentation involved feeding one or more lead pellets to caught-up wild mallard. These pellets were fed to the experimental birds mixed into a number of different diets, because some foodstuffs pass through the gut more quickly than others and may thus carry pellets safely through. The results were somewhat inconclusive, with different groups recording rather different findings. For example, it was found that feeding one No.4 pellet resulted in a mortality of 18-20% (*Longue et al 1974*). But only two years later Sales and Irwin (1976) found that there was no mortality when the same amount of lead was administered with any one of three different diets. Bellrose demonstrated that when mallard trapped on migration were fed one No.6 pellet and then released, their subsequent dispersal was not significantly different from that of untreated birds.

In addition to the clearly inconclusive nature of these findings, it is also pertinent to consider the fate of spent pellets when they fall on wetlands. Do they remain on the bed of the water and so stay available to wildfowl? Or do they sink into the underlying mud or silt and so cease to pose a threat? Much, it would seem, depends upon the movement, if any, of the water. As a general rule the more turbulence there is, so the better the chance of the pellets getting buried and out of harm's way. Many of the major die-offs that have been recorded took place in areas in which there were broad, shallow waters with little or no flow. I am personally inclined to wonder just how long pellets actually remain available to wildfowl. Lead is a particularly dense metal and logic would suggest that it would, in most cases, sink beneath the surface of the mud quite quickly.

Appropriate legislation against lead shot?

Much of this debate is, however, now merely academic. Legislation against lead has been enacted in England and Scotland despite the fact that no one really knows whether the problem of lead poisoning is significant or not in Britain. Various guesstimates have been published but, realistically, there is no way of knowing the numbers of ducks that succumb to lead poisoning. Sick birds tend to skulk in cover and following their deaths the remains are quickly removed by scavengers. Other than in the case of road casualties, how often does one come across a dead bird in the wilds? Or, for that matter, how often when flighting a wetland does one's dog bring back a dead or injured bird other than the one that has just been shot?

In England, in my view, the legislation has gone over the top and one can only hope that at some future date there will be some degree of repeal. Wishful thinking? As matters presently stand one cannot use lead shot against ducks, geese, golden plovers, moorhens, coots and snipe irrespective of where one is shooting. Quite honestly I am very glad that

Coot (left) and moorhens – among the many species for which lead shot is outlawed

I live in Ireland as snipe and golden plover provide me with a lot of sport. And I can safely say that over 90% of my bag of these two species is shot in places where there is little or no surface water and which ducks do not frequent. In the case of moorhens and coots I cannot offer comment as I have never shot either of them. In my lifetime there has not been a tradition of shooting them in Ireland. I cannot imagine that they are very good to eat. I am reminded of the story about how to deal with a shot moorhen, or water hen as they are called in Ireland. First it should be well boiled. Then it should be slowly roasted. Finally, see if the dog will chance it.

US legislation on lead shot

In North America regulations are equally restrictive. For example, Article 15(1)(b) of the Canadian Migratory Birds Convention Act, 1994 outlaws the use of lead shot for migratory bird hunting other than in the case of woodcock, band-tailed pigeon and morning doves. Even these exceptions do not apply when one is hunting in National Wildlife Areas.

Scottish laws

The situation in Scotland is rather more sensible. One is only restricted to the use of non-toxic shot for hunting ducks and geese on wetlands. In the case of geese the great majority of greylags and pinkfoot are shot over stubbles or grass where lead pellets do not cause a problem.

Ireland

At the time of writing there has been no legislation proposed in Ireland. There is certainly no compelling evidence to suggest that duck populations are threatened by the accumulation of lead in wetlands. I researched the situation in the late 1980s and found only a single area in the country which approached what our American colleagues call a 'hotspot'. A major problem for Irish legislators is the fact that there is no proof house in Ireland in which hunters could get their guns checked for their suitability to withstand the higher breech pressures generated by many of the cartridges loaded with non-toxic shot. Strangely, for a country usually quick to adapt to the thinking within the European Community, there has been no move in relation to a proof house. As far as I am aware there has not been one in the country for fifty years. Despite this, the days of lead shot for wildfowl shooting in Ireland are inevitably numbered. Sentiment rather than hard scientific fact will decide the issue. The only question is, when?

Alternatives to lead shot

With the demise of lead, non-toxic alternatives had to be found. Easier said than done. As we have seen, lead's density and softness are such that no other metal is in the same league for ballistic purposes. A number of alternatives have been tried, many of which are based on tungsten. North America has been the leader in the quest for alternatives to lead and I can do no better than take the definition of non-toxic shot written into the Migratory Bird Regulations which relate to the North American Migratory Bird Convention. Non-toxic shot is defined as steel shot, tin shot, bismuth shot, tungsten-iron shot, tungsten-matrix shot and tungsten polymer shot. Very recently, other tungsten-based shot has appeared on the market.

Steel shot

Steel shot, if for no other reason than its ready availability and relatively low cost, quickly became the main alternative to lead. Steel, strictly, is something of a misnomer. Steel is a very hard alloy produced by adding a small amount of carbon to iron. Such hardness renders it ill-suited to the matter at hand. Inter alia it would tend to pass through tissues rather than cause death by impact. In the present context, steel really means the softest available iron.

But it is still not without its drawbacks. In comparison to lead it is still relatively hard. As a result there is the possibility of damage to the lining of gun barrels as the shot charge passes through. Fortunately this problem has been largely overcome by the use of thick plastic cup-shaped wads which prevent the shot from coming into contact with the barrels. Unresolved however is the possibility of bulging if a steel charge is fired through a tightly choked barrel. Realistically there is no answer to this one and, in consequence, it is inadvisable to use steel shot in barrels that are tighter than half choke.

Another problem with steel stems from its lower density (7.9g/cm^3) which is only approximately 70% of that of lead. To achieve a comparable striking force it is therefore necessary to generate a greater breech pressure, something which effectively rules out many older guns and high quality game guns for duck shooting. Bigger pellets are also necessary to compensate for steel's lower density. The general rule of thumb is to use two sizes larger than would normally be selected in the case of lead. Thus, for example, No.5 steel equates to No.7 lead. This appears to work quite well and North American goose hunters seem to be able to bring down their quarry at similar ranges to those when they were using lead.

Tin shot

Tin, like lead, is a soft metal. Unfortunately its density (7.3g/cm^3) is even less than that of steel. Again therefore, higher breech pressures are necessary and correspondingly bigger pellets must be used. My personal experience with tin has been confined to shooting clays. For this purpose it appears to perform quite adequately but I will have to confess to reservations about firing tin at high flying ducks. With a density of less than two thirds that of lead I feel that the chances of a clean kill would be significantly reduced other than at comparatively short range.

Bismuth

Bismuth, it is generally agreed, is the best presently available alternative to lead. It is nearly as dense (9.8g/cm^3) and, despite being a little on the brittle side, has been shown to perform well in the field. The main disadvantage is one of cost. Bismuth is not a very plentiful element in the earth's crust and a ton of ore yields only a tiny amount of the metal. It constitutes 0.2 parts per million of the earth's crust as opposed to 13 parts per million in the case of lead. Iron, it may be noted, leaves these two metals in the shade when it comes to a question of relative abundance. It constitutes 50,000 parts per million of the earth's crust.

Tungsten

The remaining metal is tungsten. It is nearly twice as dense as lead (19.4g/cm^3) but it is far too hard to be used by itself. In consequence a number of modifications have been produced which are softer than the pure metal. They are also much less dense. Tungsten-iron is an alloy containing 45% iron and 55% tungsten. It may also contain tiny traces of other elements. Tungsten-matrix is a mixture of tungsten, nickel, iron and a compound with the unlikely name of ethylene methacrylic acid. Tungsten is an expensive metal and tungsten-matrix shot is probably the most expensive of all the lead alternatives. It has approximately the same density as lead and has similar ballistic properties. As is the case with steel, tungsten-matrix pellets are enclosed within a thick plastic cup to avoid barrel damage. There would appear to be some problem with these pellets when they are fired through a tightly choked barrel. At least some of them disintegrate so that the shot patterns can be rather variable. Finally there is tungsten-polymer which is composed of 93% tungsten and 7% nylon. I have never succeeded in obtaining cartridges loaded with it so I can offer no comment. Tungsten-based shot is finding ever-increasing favour with duck hunters, especially those who shoot beyond the seawall.

Losses due to crippling

Crippling losses are an unfortunate reality when it comes to shooting fast-flying birds. They occur when birds are struck by pellets but keep going, only to die later of their injuries. There are two likely scenarios that can result in crippling losses. The first is when, often as a result of a shot being fired at long range, none of the pellets find a vital organ or have sufficient momentum to bring the bird down in the hunter's immediate vicinity. The second is when stray pellets from the shot charge directed at one member of a pack strike another bird. This is especially likely to happen in the case of birds such as teal and golden plover which are given to travelling in quite tight formations. In this latter case a malformed pellet or one deformed as a result of its passage through a tightly choked barrel can deviate considerably from the centre of the pattern.

I am far from convinced that the first scenario is anything like as common as is sometimes suggested. In my experience one is nearly always aware when a bird that does not fall has been struck. The important thing is to keep watching it as, more often than not, it will eventually tail down. And this means disciplining oneself not to fire at a second bird under such circumstances. I can recall a number of occasions with duck, grouse and snipe when I saw a bird eventually fall but, in each case, the man who fired the shot was blissfully ignorant of the fact that it had found its mark. In one memorable case it was a young man's first grouse and when I came across to him sitting disconsolately in the heather he was fully convinced that he had missed a fairly simple bird with both barrels. Duck, in particular, in my experience require a lot of watching as they can carry quite a distance before collapsing.

In situations in which one is taking a bird from a pack it is doubly important to watch the survivors. Stray pellets are prone to do the most

After the flight: a good bag of mallard, well-retrieved by the gundogs

outrageous things. Once, when I was very young and still confined to a single barrelled weapon of dubious vintage, a pair of mallard crossed fairly high at the edge of a belt of floodwater. There was a lot of daylight between the two birds. And I mean a lot, several feet at least. The drake fell to my shot and I waded out into the floodwater to retrieve it. Then, as I was straightening up with my prize in my hand, my eyes picked up a flickering movement on the mud at the far side of the water. The movement was that of the duck's orange paddles. She was lying on her back and as dead as a maggot when I reached her. The extraordinary thing was that I never saw her fall.

On another occasion, by which time I had graduated to a double barrelled gun, I was presented with what was for me a very rare opportunity. A mixed pack of wigeon and pintail, some forty birds in all, came in over a reed bed in which I was concealed. They appeared well spread out as they descended open-winged towards the adjoining water. I succeeded with a not too difficult right and left, two pintail drakes, an adult majestic in full plumage and a young bird still getting its colours. Watching the survivors depart I was more than amazed to see one, then a second and finally a third bird drop. Two of them, a pintail and a wigeon, were later picked up. Of the third there was no trace.

The moral of these stories is I think clear: stray pellets are always likely to bring down birds other than the targeted ones. What is less clear is how many come down out of visual range. I have seen figures published in North America which estimate crippling losses to be as high as 35% of the retrieved bag. Unlike the US population figures, which are obtained scientifically, these I view with more than passing suspicion. How can they possibly be obtained? As is the case with mortality resulting from the ingestion of lead shot there is literally no way of ascertaining the actual number of dead birds. Moreover, being something of a cynic, I would be of the view that the suppliers of such estimates are not exactly ardent supporters of hunting. That there are crippling losses, there is no doubt. But a lifetime of shooting all manner of game birds and wildfowl under all sorts of conditions tells me that they are a much less significant cause of mortality than some would have us believe. This being said, it still behoves all of us who hunt to make every effort to ensure that every bird

Closely-grouped flocks of mallard like this are more susceptible to being struck by stray pellets and thus potentially adding to the 'crippling loss' statistics.

that is claimed to have been hit is accounted for.

My main reason for believing that crippling losses are lower than is often suggested relates to the very nature of lead as a projectile. When lead pellets strike a bird they cause, most usually, serious damage. In this context I am assuming that the hunter is firing a shot size appropriate for his quarry. Even if only two or three pellets make contact, the force of that contact is generally such as to prevent the bird from travelling far. I am firmly of the view that, in the great majority of cases, a wounded bird falls within a few hundred yards rather than a mile away.

As I have only a little experience of hunting with non-toxic alternatives to lead my thoughts in relation to crippling losses must be based largely on the theoretical. I would have some concerns with tin and steel because of the lower densities of these two metals. In the case of steel these concerns have not been helped by film that I have seen in which it was being used against Canada geese. In one film in particular, in which the geese were being decoyed into stubbles, there were few clean kills despite what had every appearance of close range shooting. And in a number of instances it took more than one shot to bring the goose down.

I think that the fact that steel is harder than lead does not help either. As a consequence of its hardness it is more likely to pass through a bird's tissues than generate the shock on impact which brings the bird down even when no vital organ has been struck. There is also the point that the use of larger pellets means that the gun throws less reliable patterns. This is not to say that larger pellets should not be used. As already mentioned they are a necessary compensation for lower density. What it does mean is that the hunter must exercise far greater restraint when it comes to target range. For inland duck shooting this is unlikely to be a major problem as most shots are taken at well under forty yards. Often, indeed, at less than thirty.

Coastal shooting is another matter. On those all too frequent cold, still mornings when ducks are up in the clouds I would have reservations about the use of low density shot even when propelled with greater ferocity. This, I think, is a situation which could lead to a serious level of crippling losses. Bismuth, with its greater density, or Tungsten-based shot, would appear to be more appropriate under such conditions.

CHAPTER SEVEN

REGULATIONS

Significant differences exist between the sets of regulations governing the activities of duck hunters on either side of the Atlantic. In some cases these differences merely reflect different traditions. But in other cases some very good reasons can be found to explain them. Chief amongst these is one for which much credit must go to all those concerned with migratory bird hunting in North America. Essentially they make every effort to tie the hunting 'take' in any one year to the ebb and flow of the fortunes of the different quarry species. Whilst accepting that this endeavour involves no small degree of uncertainty, so complex are the factors that dictate population trends, there is a lot that we can learn from them. More on this later.

Another reason for the differences in regulations relates to the sheer size of the North American continent, stretching from the frozen wastes of the High Arctic down almost to the equator, and to the countless numbers of wild ducks that live there. Essentially, for any given species, numbers may be very high in one part of that great continent and very low in another. And, because of the enormity of the annual migration, numbers can differ significantly in a given area as the days of autumn pass.

Rights to foreshore shooting

Then there is the fact that, whereas in Britain and Ireland most duck hunting takes place on private property, in North America a lot of people hunt over lands that are in public ownership. In our islands the nearest we have to areas in public ownership is the foreshore. But even here matters are anything but straightforward, especially in England and Wales. First of all there is no uniformity of definition as to what exactly is meant by the foreshore. This need not concern us greatly. For practical purposes we are talking about the area outside the seawall which is subject to being covered/exposed according to the state of the tide. In England and Wales much of the foreshore belongs to the Crown or to the Duchy of Lancaster. The rest is in public ownership. It would appear that there is no automatic right to hunt on Crown/Duchy of Lancaster foreshores. However, the British Association for Shooting and Conservation (BASC) has helped constituent wildfowling clubs to acquire leases over many of these areas. In Scotland the situation is very different and a lot more democratic. Members of the public have the right to shoot over the foreshore other than in areas which have been set aside as national reserves or parks. For some strange reason this freedom to hunt on the foreshore does not extend to the islands of Orkney and Shetland.

In Ireland the situation concerning the foreshore is different again. Prior to 1976, duck hunters could shoot over the foreshore without let or hindrance. But then, following the passage into law of the Wildlife Act in that year, it became necessary to obtain a permit. Except where reserves exist, or in a very limited number of places where demand is very high, this can be obtained without difficulty. There is no charge. A similar permit is necessary to shoot over the country's great lakes such as those of the Shannon system.

The main regulations governing duck hunting concern the appointment of open seasons and related matters. In Britain the 1981 Wildlife and Countryside Act is the relevant instrument. The 1976 Wildlife Act is its equivalent in Ireland. In North America the agreement signed between the United States and Canada in 1916 forms the basis for both federal and state/provincial legislation in the two countries. Called the Migratory Birds Convention, it is a most forward-looking document from an era in which conservation was not generally treated with anything like its present importance. Some twenty years on Mexico became a signatory to the convention thus introducing uniformity over the continent. The convention was updated and amended in 2004.

Wild duck shooting seasons

In Britain the season for wild duck shooting runs from 1 September to 31 January of the following year. Additionally shooting is permissible until 20 February at any point below the mean high water level of ordinary spring tides. In Ireland the season also runs from 1 September to 31 January. Until about thirty years ago there was an extension for species other than mallard. This, presumably, was on the basis that the great majority of other species were migratory and that, unlike the mallard, were nowhere near turning their minds to thoughts of procreation.

In England and Wales there is little uniformity in relation to shooting wildfowl on Sundays. Counties as far apart as Devon and Yorkshire ban the practice as do many of the Welsh counties. Regulations in Scotland are very different. It is illegal to shoot wildfowl in any part of the country on Sunday but the same prohibition does not apply to game. In fact game can in theory be shot on Christmas day. However, should one wish to shoot game on a Sunday it is accepted practice that one does not do so until church services have concluded around midday. Matters are very different in Ireland and reflect a very different shooting tradition. In Ireland shooting is very much everyman's sport and Sunday is the most usual day for a hunting trip.

Under the terms of the Migratory Birds Convention, the contracting parties agreed to, and enshrined in their federal legislation, a close season for migratory birds from 10 March to 1 September. However this does not mean that hunting is permissible for the rest of the year. Any one season is restricted to a maximum of 14 weeks. Each of the contracting parties is to decide the period(s) outside the close season when hunting is most appropriate in different parts of their countries. Such factors as the timing and pathways of migration will influence the decision-making processes. For example, the duck hunting season in the Northern Zone of Labrador runs from the first Saturday in September until the second Saturday of

This female eider would do well to avoid the Northern Zone in October

December whereas in the Southern Zone it begins on the second Saturday of September and runs to the third Saturday of December.

In Labrador a more profound difference exists between the two zones in the case of hunting eider ducks (sea ducks are generally treated as a separate category in North America. The term is used to cover, where applicable, eiders, scoters and long-tailed ducks). In the Northern Zone the eider season commences on the last Saturday of September whereas in the Southern Zone it is delayed until the fourth Sunday of November.

The Canadian provincial authorities tend to allow somewhere near the maximum 3½ months hunting seasons for ducks. Sometimes though an individual province may opt for a shorter season. Presently, for example, the main duck hunting season in Manitoba only runs from 8th September to 30th November.

Across the United States, seasons can vary widely from state to state, again reflective of migratory patterns and climatic differences. It is also not uncommon to find the season divided into a number of separate phases.

Virginia, for example, allows a 60 day season which, for 2006/07 was divided into three: 5 October to 9 October, 18 November to 2 December and 9 December to 27 January. A similar arrangement applies in Florida where the 2006/07 season is about the same length and again divided into three. But here life gets even more complicated. It is broken up into a short early season for wood ducks and teal (blue-winged and green-winged, the former in particular being amongst the first ducks to move south in autumn). This is from 23 September to 27 September. The regular season then runs from 18 November to 26 November and from 9 December to 28 January.

In comparison to their American and Canadian counterparts, it can be seen that British and Irish hunters face far fewer restrictions. Year after year the timing and duration of seasons tend to remain the same. The only real interruption comes in the form of a temporary closure should severe weather descend. Effectively severe weather means that a majority of weather stations have recorded the ground remaining frozen for 13 days. Under the terms of the Wildlife and Countryside Act the Secretary of State is then empowered to introduce a 14-day shooting ban in respect of all wildfowl. Similar provisions are to be found in the Irish Wildlife Act. Here the relevant Minister (responsibility for wildlife changes from time to time) is empowered to bring in a ban of up to 28 days for all or part of the country.

Hours of shooting

Two major restrictions are an integral part of the North American hunting scene. They relate to the hours during which it is permissible to shoot wildfowl and the number of birds that may be killed in a day.

In contrast, no such restrictions exist in Britain and Ireland. We can shoot ducks throughout the 24 hours. Dusk and dawn are the most favoured periods. Indeed it is more or less certain that the greater part of the annual bag is taken at the hour of dusk. For many duck enthusiasts the nights surrounding the full moon have a very special attraction as birds are on the wing on and off throughout the night.

On this point there is a school of thought that believes that moon flighting should be outlawed on the basis that the ducks are deprived of an adequate opportunity to feed. Personally I do not think that this is a serious issue as the wigeon simply move off when disturbed and find alternative feeding. Anyway there are usually only a handful of nights each month when conditions, especially the right cloud cover, are suitable.

In sharp contrast, in North America wildfowl shooting is only permissible during the period starting one half hour before sunrise and ending at sunset. Quite clearly then there is no evening flighting as we know it. Even dawn flighting is limited, especially under cloudless skies, as many ducks will have gone about their business before the appointed time.

Daily bag limits

Daily bag limits have long been part of the North American hunting tradition. Their purpose is admirable. In theory they provide a means of protecting those species whose numbers are down by shifting the shooting pressure towards those that are more plentiful. Quite clearly a high degree of hunter discipline is essential. Equally the hunter must be proficient in the matter of bird identification. In this respect it is entirely logical to confine shooting to the hours of daylight. It is virtually impossible to be 100% certain of the identity of every duck that comes into range in the twilight hours. On a number of occasions down the years I thought that I had a wigeon down at dusk, only for the dog to present me with a shoveler.

As already noted, the daily bag limit can change from year to year according to the changing fortunes of the various species. To get an idea of the sheer complexity of the US system the following are operative at the time of writing. As different states/provinces operate differently it is first necessary to subdivide into a number of categories. Those states that allow an early (September) season restrict the quarry to teal and, in some cases, wood ducks. North Carolina, Florida and Texas are examples. In each of these states the bag limit is four. In Florida no more than two of them may be wood ducks. In North Carolina blue-winged teal, green-winged teal and cinnamon teal may all be shot.

Matters now get even more complicated. In addition to the conventional or regular bag, effectively composed of dabbling and diving ducks, there may be a second daily limit for sea ducks and a third for mergansers.

To further complicate the issue these latter two categories are sometimes lumped together.

Taking Canada first, Newfoundland allows a daily bag of 6 for each of the three categories ie 6 regular, 6 sea ducks and 6 mergansers whereas Labrador allows 6 for the regular bag and a further 6 for sea ducks and mergansers combined.

Moving to the United States, Oregon and New York State have single daily limits of 7 and 6 respectively and mergansers are included in these. Florida includes sea ducks in its regular limit of 6. Across North America 6 is the most common bag limit. Canada is a little more generous than the United States with five provinces allowing 8. Up in the North West Territories and Nunavut the figure rises to 25, presumably a recognition of the importance of this form of animal protein to the people of the regions.

Within the daily limits it is not unusual to find species limits and sex limits. These can be quite complex and the hunter must really have his wits about him before lining up an individual duck. Take as an example the regulations in Virginia. This state has one of the lowest daily limits (5) qualified as follows; no more than 4 mallard (which may include no more than 2 hens), 2 scaup, 2 wood ducks, 2 redheads, 1 pintail, 1 mottled duck, 1 black duck (except during the period 5–9 October) and 1 canvasback. Texas is not too dissimilar. Here the daily limit is 6 but with the following provisos, no more than 5 mallard (which may include not more than two hens), 2 scaup, 2 wood ducks, 2 redheads, 1 'dusky' duck (mottled duck, black duck or Mexican duck), 1 pintail, 1 canvasback. Texas also has a merganser limit of 5 of which only one may be a hooded merganser.

I have often wondered how we would fare here in the face of regulations such as these. I have more than a suspicion that the relevant custodians of law and order would have to be on their toes if such were introduced. Of course evening flighting and moon flighting would have to go. I have no doubt that there would be rather more than token resistance if officialdom tried to impose such a regime on us. As matters presently stand in both Britain and Ireland I think that it is fair to argue that there is no real need for bag limits. It is only on comparatively rare occasions that the duck hunter gets the opportunity to shoot a lot of ducks. Most of us can look back on a positive litany of blank flights. Usually anything in excess of three or four birds represents a good evening.

Baiting for duck

Another major difference between the two traditions concerns what is called baiting in North America. Essentially we are talking about putting out grain or other food to attract wildfowl to a particular stretch of water. With very few exceptions, and indeed the acquisition of a permit (something not easily obtained), the practice is outlawed there. Here, in sharp contrast, it is almost routine for many of us. Two or three times a week, at least, I scatter a generous number of fistfuls of barley in the shallows of the ponds on our farm. Contrast this with the situation in Canada. There it is illegal to hunt wildfowl within 400 metres of a place unless it has been free of bait for 7 days. In the United States the period is ten days. Moreover, it is still a violation of the law even if the hunter is unaware that bait had been laid in a particular place.

Youth Waterfowl Days

The hunting regulations in North America are clearly much more restrictive than those that govern our sport here. However I want to end this chapter with mention of one provision in those regulations that is anything but restrictive. It relates to the appointment of one or more days, according to the state, which are given the name of Youth Waterfowl Days. They are set aside for young people of 15 or younger, down to 12 in some states, to hunt wildfowl. Most commonly these appointed days are outside the regular duck season. The youth, who must be accompanied by an adult licence holder, is entitled to shoot up to the normal bag limit. The accompanying adult is generally not allowed to shoot on that day unless it falls within the regular duck season. I think that this is a very positive concept. Maybe we should institute something similar here during the period immediately following the end of the season.

CHAPTER EIGHT

WALKING UP DUCKS

First of all I must explain precisely what I mean by walking up. In the broadest and most obvious sense, the term is used to describe the shooting of game which the guns themselves have flushed with or without the assistance of dogs. In the days when the grey partridge was plentiful, walking up involved a line of guns, no more then thirty or forty yards apart, traversing such likely spots as high and weedy stubbles, turnips and potatoes. They (the partridges) never seemed to have much regard for beet. I suspect that it was too enclosed and damp for their liking. We rarely used to meet them in beet unless they were taking cover there, having been first flushed elsewhere. Dogs played no part in the proceedings other than to walk obediently behind the line and retrieve on command. It is in this narrow sense that I use the term walking up. Essentially it is the sportsman and not his canine companion that is doing the flushing.

In passing it is worthy of note that snipe are ideal candidates for this form of shooting as they are not inclined to stay on the ground when humanity invades their patch. Not for them the cowardly practice of grouse and pheasants of scuttling away and skulking in dense vegetation. It is simply a matter of up and away, uttering that sharp screech as soon as they become aware of one's presence. But they can be unpredictable. One day they will sit relatively tight, on another they will rise two gunshots out. For me it is this lack of predictability which provides the great challenge of snipe shooting. Whilst one tends to know the most likely spots, the reality is that they can get up anywhere. One's concentration must never be allowed to wander. Following some utterly perverse rule of Nature, it is at the very moment that the mind strays from the job in hand that snipe insist upon taking to the air. How much easier is dogging. First there is the change in behaviour when a bird is scented. Then there is the point. No excuses concerning momentary lapses of concentration are acceptable now.

Woodcock, too, can be walked up without dogs but usually with rather less success because of the very different surroundings. The noise that one makes breaking through the cover is usually sufficient to get them airborne. But the guns need to be fairly close together to ensure that none are left behind, especially if the cover is heavy. Many sportsmen assume that woodcock always make their escape by the aerial route but this is not necessarily the case. On several occasions I have seen them legging it at fair speed from one patch of brambles or furze to the next. To be honest though, I have no idea how frequently they use plan B.

I am told that where grouse are plentiful they can be flushed by a line of guns. However I cannot vouch for this as the places in which I pursue these magnificent birds hold but few. Without good dogs on top form and good scenting conditions, one could walk a long mile without seeing as much as a single bird. We would regard a bag of two or three as a more than fair day on the hill.

Once, many years ago, I was invited to a walked up hare shoot in Cambridgeshire. Coming from a part of the world where hares are not shot (they are regarded as the sport of the coursing fraternity) I had mixed feelings about taking up the invitation. Eventually I did. It was not an experience that I would wish to repeat. Maybe it was just that I was not prepared for the events that were to unfold. Suffice to say that, so numerous were the hares, the number shot was quite extraordinary. By evening the broad fields of the farms on which we were shooting reminded me of a battleground. Since that day I have only once shot a hare. This was at the request of an old Polish friend who had expressed a desire for one which he wanted to cook in some traditional way.

Since, like snipe, ducks tend to insist upon an immediate departure at the slightest hint of human presence they too are ideal candidates for walking up. But sometimes tactics have to be varied. One situation may require a combination of walking up and an impromptu drive. Then again, there are times when what started as walking up evolves into a form of flighting, as birds that perversely rise out of range decide to throw caution to the wind and return. In such mad moments men have been known to throw themselves with alacrity into whatever patch of cover happens to be available.

The main difficulty facing anyone who wants to walk up ducks is obtaining access to a sufficiently large area for the purpose. Moreover the area must, ideally, contain a lot of small and well-spaced wet places or, at least, a lengthy stretch of river. If one's shooting territory only has a pond or two, much better sport is likely to be obtained by using them for flighting. There is precious little point in walking up to a pond and shooting one or two of its departing occupants if a sensible feeding programme can deliver several times this number every fortnight or so. For practical purposes, walked up duck shooting can be divided into two scenarios. The first of these centres upon moving waters, anything from small streams to rivers. The second centres on ponds, drains and other such places where there is little or no water flow. In both cases there is the same proviso. It is the same as that which applies to a shoot with a limited amount of water. If any of these places are attracting a flight of ducks, be it at dawn or dusk, one should think twice before deciding upon the optimum shooting regime.

In my experience, streams and small rivers are 'safe' places for walking up ducks: safe in the sense that they do not usually provide much in the way of flighting opportunities. A few ducks may come in at dusk but they can alight at any point so that any attempt at an ambush is little more than a lottery. I know of streams which have stretches all but guaranteed to show a bundle of mallard in the early morning. But waiting at dusk at the spots where they usually rise is a waste of time. A few may pass over high or one may hear that magical whispering of wings in the darkness. And that

Waiting by the river while the other gun flushes out the quarry from round the bend upstream.

is about it. I suspect that they pitch in at various points, usually upstream of the preferred feeding area, and then cruise down to it as evening gives way to night. The one exception is those lovely streams which break out into ponds or marshy patches in the course of their meanderings. They provide something of a dilemma, especially as winter progresses and the night frosts become more severe. It is quite surprising how many ducks, in particular teal, will come into a pond supplied by running water when the temperature drops to the wrong side of zero.

There is a section of the mountains where we shoot grouse, probably best described as foothills, where a tiny stream bubbles out of the peat and flows a couple of miles down to the valley. We walk it once or twice a year after a day at the grouse. It has yet to yield as much as a solitary duck; at best it may grudgingly produce a few snipe when the first migrants touch down in September. But, at three points, each no more than fifty yards from the next, it broadens out into what may just about be described as ponds.

They are surprisingly deep, one in particular is both very deep and very treacherous. None of them seems to be particularly well-endowed with vegetation. Indeed they appear to be quite typical of the duck-unfriendly waters that are so often found on acids peats. But duck-unfriendly they are not. At dusk on a mid-September evening there is no finer spot to round off an afternoon on the hill. We usually try to arrive at these ponds about twenty minutes before dusk. With luck there will be a scattering of brownish feathers at the edges and a few more sailing on the water. Once in a fairly long while we get a bag that runs into double figures. More usually though, four or five mallard provide a more than ample return for the wait. Strangely, they rarely come in October. I can only assume that whatever food the ponds provide gets exhausted during September.

We had one most unusual experience at these ponds which is worth recounting. Or, to be strictly accurate, my partner had the unusual experience. It was a Saturday evening late in September and there had been a good flight. Somewhere approaching a dozen mallard were shot. Most of them had been safely retrieved but when we took our leave of the place in inky blackness we felt that there were one or two that had not been accounted for. I was unable to return the following morning so it was left to my partner to give his springer an opportunity to complete the pick up. When he arrived at the scene shortly after dawn he was amazed to see nearly fifty mallard standing motionless in a wet and rushy area about one hundred yards from the ponds. What they were doing there after the hammering of the previous evening is a mystery. It was the only occasion on which we were aware of mallard being present during the hours of daylight. It would be nice to record that he walked over and took a pair as they lifted. Alas, this was not the case. However he, or more correctly his springer, succeeded in finding two of the slain.

Walking up early morning streams

Streams are generally feeding (as opposed to roosting) places. They are, in consequence, best walked up in the very early morning as ducks tend to move off at about the time the world is waking up. Rivers are rather different and, in so saying, I am aware of the very real difficulty of distinguishing a stream from a river. When a river is broad enough to deserve

Small ponds such as this with very little cover are best shot at dusk.

its title it may be used for feeding or for roosting during the hours of daylight. If it is located in an undisturbed area it may serve both roles, especially in the early part of the shooting season. Mallard broods, undisturbed since late spring, tend to remain faithful to a stretch of the river unless something untoward happens. This, in the main, means unseasonable rains that transform the river into a roaring red torrent which leaves the ducks with no alternative than to seek temporary alternative accommodation.

In this part of the country where I have spent most of my life, the smaller rivers are characterised by long shallow stretches interspersed with still, deep pools. In late summer, water levels are normally at their lowest and the shallow stretches are adorned with numerous weed-covered reddish sandbanks. It is on these that the mallard broods laze away their days. A liberal scattering of feathers and an assortment of droppings bear silent witness to the most favoured sandbanks. By 1st September these small rivers provide walked up shooting par excellence for those who get there first on that sacred morning.

After the first September onslaught, the ducks will, unsurprisingly, spend rather less of their time on those favoured stretches. From now on, being fast learners, they will tend increasingly to feed in one place and roost in another unless disturbance levels are minimal. This change in behaviour has important implications in so far as shooting is concerned. If the river provides good feeding, walking up in the early morning is indicated. But if it is mainly used for roosting there is no necessity to drag oneself from a warm bed at the crack of dawn. They will be there all day so one can pay a visit at a more civilised hour.

The secret therefore, is to know one's rivers and what they have to offer for ducks. In other words: are they primarily used for roosting or feeding? There are certain giveaways. If, for example, a river is small and weedy it is, in all probability, a place which duck will visit at dusk. But if it has a bare, stony bed and quieter waters under the banks, it is most likely to be used for roosting. There is such a river about ten miles from here. It tumbles down from the hills only to lose much of its energy as the gradient flattens. At one point where it flows serenely, there is an island generously endowed with sallies. Behind this island, which is no more than a couple of hundred square yards in extent, lies a quiet backwater. Like the rest of the river this backwater is scarcely two feet in depth. By November most of our migrant teal have taken up residence and some of them spend their days on the backwater. More often than not they are in the company of a few mallard. When disturbed the assembled ducks have no option other than a vertical ascent because of the density of the surrounding sallies. Our technique, if technique is the right term, is quite straightforward. We simply wade out quietly into the river and lob a stone over the island. Most times an assortment of splashing and quacking means that we have struck lucky.

Roosting places

Still and deep stretches of a river suggest the possibility of a roosting place, especially if there is a muddy bank overhung with bushes. Once one gets to know a particular river, the favoured roosting spots become apparent. Then, armed with this knowledge, a plan of campaign can be devised. Sometimes the plan will involve a drive. Two circumstances lend themselves to such a course of action. The first is when the river bends. Duck, when flushed, tend to follow the course of the river for the first few hundred yards or so. As a result, it makes good sense to position a gun just below the bend. Once he is suitably concealed at his ambush point, his partner walks slowly along the bank so that any ducks present see him at a distance and take wing with a minimum of alarm.

One river that we shoot in particular lends itself to this procedure. It runs slow and deep for about six hundred yards before turning abruptly to the left. The far bank for much of the six hundred yards supports an ancient grove of Scots Pine. So high are the trees that the ducks, whether they like it or not, have little option other than to follow the river once disturbed. The bank that we walk is fairly open but has a few clusters of bushes under which the ducks tend to roost. As long as the place is not shot too often, the man lying in ambush can count himself most unlucky if he does not get more than a fair chance at a right and left. As a general rule it is better if the 'beater' does not fire, as suddenly and dramatically disturbed ducks can fly off in any direction. This though is really a matter of personal preference.

In dry autumns this particular stretch really comes into its own. Whilst mallard and teal are almost invariably present, they are joined by wigeon as they begin to filter inland. The shooting is great until the winter floods arrive. After that it is more profitable to seek ducks elsewhere during the hours of daylight. Two years ago we had little rain until late November with the exception of a cloudburst in October that provided a scattering of short-lived flashes. These were just sufficient to lure the wigeon from the sea which is about twenty miles away. One of my sons and I walked/ ambushed the river early one November morning. As the senior member of the partnership I do the ambushing and he does the walking. The form is that I take a wide circle and creep into a cluster of bushes conveniently situated just round the bend. Then, and only then, he and his springer set off. On this particular morning I was barely in position when a couple of shots rang out. As indicated earlier, it is preferable that the 'beater' does not fire. But this was a unique occasion. Never before had we seen such a company of ducks lift from the river. As soon as he set out, mallard, wigeon and teal were rising all along the river. At least one hundred ducks and probably considerably more were moving in all directions. The wigeon, not comprehending what was expected of them, came nowhere near me. The mallard however obliged and I was rewarded with a fine pair of drakes. Walking back along the bank I found the son out in the field with a wigeon in hand. He was busily searching for a second which had planed down but, despite the best efforts of his springer Willow, it was never found. This was unusual as Willow rarely misses a bird so we could only conclude that it had got up again.

The second possibility for driving a river is where the bank has a dense growth of bushes for quite a distance and the water is relatively shallow. The river described above has such a stretch about a mile upstream which, by incredibly good fortune, is owned by a brother-in-law of mine. A positive thicket of blackthorns along the bank has two gaps most conveniently situated about one hundred yards apart. One gun circles around and walks in slowly towards the gap that lies further downstream. He then stands about ten yards back from the bank.

Look for the likely roosting places during a daytime reconnaissance of the river. Armed with this knowledge your plan of campaign can be devised

Once he is in position the second gun enters the river at the first gap. The river is quite shallow and he is able to wade downstream without difficulty. In this scenario there is nothing to prevent the 'beater' from firing, as the ducks have little option but to fly downstream. Usually the

DRIVING DUCK TOWARDS A BEND IN THE RIVER
B may have to take a long and circuitous route to the ambush point. A should then approach the bank slowly, and simply follow it along. He should avoid looping in and out, as suddenly startled duck are liable to break in any direction. It is usually alright to drive into a slight headwind, but success is unlikely if conditions are blustery.
In an ideal situation there would be heavy cover on the far bank so that the duck, if gently flushed, will tend to follow the course of the river.

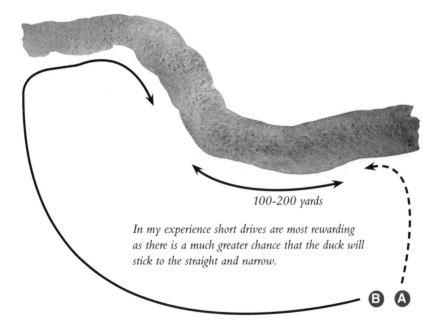

100-200 yards

In my experience short drives are most rewarding as there is a much greater chance that the duck will stick to the straight and narrow.

standing gun gets the shooting as the ducks tend to lie under the bushes quite near to where he is positioned. On those rare occasions on which the Gods smile benevolently on mankind, both the wading gun and the standing gun get a pair each.

As to actually walking up a river, there is little point in simply following the bank. Unless there is a solid wall of bushes with gaps at the right intervals, the ducks, unless they are completely half witted, will be up and gone well out of range. All that one can do in most cases is loop in and out at strategic intervals, ideally every 50–100 yards, making use of whatever cover is available on the bank. Should there be two walking guns I am generally opposed to the idea of taking a bank each. This for no better reason than safety. Teal, in particular, have an alarming habit at times of flying low and the best of us can momentarily lose contact with space and time in that instant at which a bird rises. Far better to stay on one bank and loop in simultaneously a reasonable distance apart. An exception may be made when the river is broad enough to permit safe shooting from both banks. But, realistically, such rivers rarely lend themselves to walked up shooting unless they are generously fringed with reeds.

Effects of the weather

Certain weather conditions, high wind and frost in particular, can favour shooting from the bank. There is though the inevitable proviso when it comes to the creatures of the wilds. They can have an annoying habit of ignoring the prepared script. One great advantage of wind is that it can muffle the shots. On a still day sound can travel a long way and the discharge of a couple of barrels can clear a river of its avian inhabitants for several hundred yards. But the effect of wind on the birds themselves can be unpredictable. Some days wild conditions make them a bit edgy and hard to approach. Then, in some strange form of compensation, there are the days when they are so well tucked in under overhanging branches that they are much slower than usual to rise.

One downside of a high wind is that ducks may not behave in their usual manner once airborne. Much as they may want to follow the river away from human intruders, the buffeting they receive may be such as to cause them to alter their flight course. Sometimes, having risen high and wide in the wind they will take the easy option and go back over you a couple of gunshots up.

Frost, and in particular hard and persistent frost that lasts a few days, really brings moving water into its own as far as duck shooting is concerned. Especially when one is well inland and escape to the milder surroundings of the coast is not an option for ducks in the short term. Under these conditions the smaller, weedy rivers really come into their own. They will receive a lot of evening visitations and in some cases a good flight may develop. I will deal with this in a later chapter. Despite the severe conditions walking up such places is still an early morning event. I like to be in a position to start walking as soon as there is sufficient light to see a rising bird. If one is tardy about extracting oneself from a warm and comfortable bed there is every chance that the ducks will have left to roost elsewhere.

There will always be the big letdowns. Two or three nights of sub zero temperatures which promise so much and yield so little. Maybe the ducks decided to dine elsewhere the previous evening or maybe they are where one expected them to be and the dog gets it all wrong. Most dedicated duck hunters will know the scene. Fingers frozen to the cold steel of

WALKING UP DUCK ALONG A RIVER
A and B loop in simultaneously, making use of any available cover on the bank. Where cover is available to A it is advisable for B to allow him to be a little ahead in order to maximize the chance of a shot.

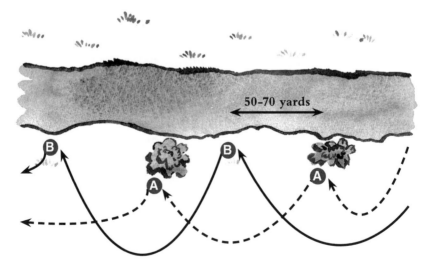

the barrels, expectations astronomical, one sets off across the glistening ground. An ever-willing spaniel will be, hopefully, at heel. I say hopefully because that same springer, mindful of his more usual role as a terroriser of woodcock, might just forget that this requires a different job description. Few things in life are more designed to turn one into the equivalent of a homicidal maniac than a dog rushing in and flushing ducks out of range. Indeed it is not unknown for threats of summary execution to be made. They are, of course, never carried out but the canine offender is given due warning that a repeat performance could have the most serious of consequences.

The single greatest problem on a frosty morning is the stillness of the air. The sounds of the first shots can carry to near eternity and result in numbers of black knobs departing in the distance at great speed. It is however advisable to make for the nearest cover in this eventuality as some of the black knobs may be disorientated and choose a flight path that brings them in range.

Whilst, on those beautiful mornings when the rest of the world is still at rest, the primary objective of one's designs are ducks, a few snipe will almost invariably enter the picture. The question is: does one shoot them or grant them safe passage in the hope of bagging a few ducks? Long and bitter experience has provided me with the answer to this one. If a snipe gets up shoot it. OK, there will be times when one watches in dismay as clusters of ducks depart quacking indignantly. But for every one of those times there will be at least one when nothing else rises and one is exceedingly grateful for the small mercy of a snipe or two.

One final word in relation to frost. In those increasingly rare instances when it persists for a week or more the quality of restraint must be applied. Wildfowl are more than capable of coping with the most adverse of conditions for a few days but, should the severity of the weather be prolonged, they will inevitably become less than worthy quarry. At this juncture there is no alternative for the inland duck shooter but to remain in the aforementioned warm and comfortable bed until a later hour and hope for the speedy return of the good times.

Walking up duck on ponds

And so to ponds. A cynic, I suppose, might possibly enquire as to whether there is much to be said or written about walking up ducks on a pond. After all, is it not merely a matter of a stealthy approach and, hopefully, a right and left from the departing inhabitants? In some cases, to be honest, the answer is in the simple affirmative. But, this being said, there are many instances when there is rather more to the matter.

First there is the pond itself. Its very nature and location will decide whether it is better suited to walking up or flighting. In some cases the optimum strategy may depend upon the time of year. A September pond bristling with reeds and other vegetation in which young and inexperienced mallard may be tempted to hide can be a very different creature in December following the combined assault of wind, rain, frost and marauding cattle. The same pond may be small or large. I know people who always refer to their large pond as a lake. Lakes, after all, are a bit more upmarket than mere ponds. Then again it may be deep or shallow. In the former case it might meet the roosting requirements of dabbling ducks. Alternatively, if it is big enough tufted ducks may come at dusk to feed.

Some ponds are spring fed, others must rely upon an accumulation of surface water to merit their title. Ponds fenced off from domestic animals quickly gather a rich flora that can be very attractive to ducks. Not just for the vegetation itself but for the myriad of small invertebrates that complement it. In contrast, where cattle have access, there may be no vegetation and the pond can take on the appearance of a muddy water hole. Most people, in referring to a pond, have in mind as isolated body of water. But some of the best shooting ponds are those which are part of a moving water system.

The reality is that the term pond covers a broad spectrum and rarely are two ponds alike. And this refers as much to their location as it does to their nature. They can be in the middle of a field or tucked away secretively in a rushy corner. They can nestle conveniently near the sea at the base of sand dunes and they can be in the middle of a wood.

Limestone ponds attract ducks

Conventional wisdom has it that ponds on limestone are preferable for wildfowl to those on acid peats. This is because the higher pH of limestone regions is conducive to the growth of a much greater range of aquatic plants. And more plants means a greater diversity of invertebrate life. There are certainly ponds and small lakes on moorland and mountain where one sees what looks like attractive habitat but where one never actually encounters as much as a single duck. I am thinking especially of places in the Scottish Highlands and in the west of Ireland. In the Irish Midlands lying next to the road from Birr to Ferbane a large area of cutaway bog was flooded some years ago as a conservation initiative. I pass it regularly and have yet to see more than a very occasional duck there. The best it seems to have on offer is the odd flock of roosting gulls. Maybe at some future date it will develop its own flora and become an attractive proposition for ducks. But somehow I have my doubts.

Collectively ponds must be the most threatened of all wildlife habitats in these islands. By the late 1950s there were parts of Britain and Ireland where they had become the inanimate equivalent of endangered species. And much worse was still to come. When, in the 1970s, we joined the then EEC, agriculture went through a period of unprecedented growth. There were places where every last rood of land was brought into productivity, often at the expense of watery places. In those days generous grants were made available for each and every reclamation project. Now, quite correctly, the grants are gone and Europe has realised belatedly that we must do all in our power to preserve such precious places.

Ideal duck ponds

In general, larger ponds have greater potential for flighting than smaller ones and are therefore best left for this. Sometimes location will decide the issue. For example, an open pond in the middle of a flat field is likely to defy any attempt at walking up and so should be left for flighting. Local knowledge is all-important. Often, for reasons best known to themselves, ducks select certain ponds for daytime roosting and flight out religiously each evening as dusk descends. In some cases these roosting ponds can appear to provide as much in the way of dabbling potential as those that are used at night for feeding. These roosting ponds tend to be located in secluded spots and, with the proviso that there is no shortage of roosts in the area, they should be the main targets for walked up shooting.

As with flighting, the essential thing is to shoot them sparingly. With experience one learns the best way of launching the assault. Much depends upon the immediate topography. With luck there will be a stout thorn hedge running up to the bank or, perhaps, a strategically situated cluster of brambles. In my experience the actual approach is rarely the problem. It is the last couple of crucial steps at the end of the cover that are apt to provide the greatest difficulty. Three of my favourite ponds will illustrate what I mean.

The first is at the end of a rushy and furzy field. The field is not large, a little short of three acres perhaps, but it is something of a wildlife paradise. It occupies the only depression in what is otherwise prime agricultural land. Because there is no real outlet for drainage it has long been abandoned to Nature. Cattle are turned in for a few weeks in the summer and they provide an invaluable service of keeping the rushes in some sort of check. The pond is easy to approach as it is shielded by a positive wall of furze. Cattle have a long-standing path through this wall which has something of a tunnel about it as the furze limbs have closed overhead. On emerging from this tunnel one is on the very edge of the pond and in full view of any residents. There is however one drawback. At the best of times the path is sticky, having been churned by count-less hooves. When the rains come it has the consistency of a quagmire. With every step one sinks a little further into the ooze. In terms of range it should be a pair of birds every time. But as is so often the case in the shooting field, theory and practice have a habit of diverging. Knocking a pair with both feet firmly anchored in the mud is no mean achievement. Good shooting has everything to do with footwork and balance.

The second pond is bisected by a very high and neglected black-thorn ditch. The ducks almost always favour one side which has a conven-iently high bank of clay jutting out into the field. This clay bank has a topping of brambles. The pond relies solely on surface water and it is usually November before much has accumulated. But once it has filled. mallard and teal are rarely absent. A great advantage because of the height of the clay bank is that one can get very near to the pond even when the brambles have died down. Then there is only plan A. Since there are just too many surrounding bushes to be sure of a successful shot when the ducks rise, it is necessary to make a rush up the clay bank. By the time one is on top of it the teal in particular are well up and provide the most challenging of shots as one attempts to steady oneself. It is only a small pond but it is very secluded and in consequence can hold a lot of ducks. On a good day it is possible to spring in excess of twenty teal and maybe half a dozen mallard.

Pond number three is a relatively big pond, over eighty yards in length, and nestles beneath two high ditches set at right angles. It is at the lower end of a long sloping field. Once again getting near poses few problems as one can creep in unseen along an adjacent hedgerow. At one corner of the pond stands an ancient oak and one is safe from view until reaching it. But as soon as one rounds the tree the ducks get up. This pond presents two difficulties. The first, once again, is the muddiness of the surrounds courtesy of the seemingly ever present cattle. This means that one is likely to get bogged down as soon as one steps out from the cover of the oak. The second is that the ducks have a most inconsiderate habit of frequenting the far end of the pond and are thus likely to rise at maximum range. Sometimes there is insufficient time for a second barrel as they are quickly out of range. Along under the surrounding ditches are dense clusters of reeds in which mallard tend to lurk. Not infrequently I have reached the oak tree, stepped around the corner and fired two quick shots at departing teal. Then I have watched in dismay as half a dozen or more mallard launched themselves casually into the air. In theory one should keep dead cool, reload and take one or two of them. But once again theory and practice have a habit of diverging. Two feet stuck firmly in the mud, fingers fumbling furiously in the pocket for cartridges and, all the while, the quacking pack is becoming a cluster of increasingly small dots.

Despite these vicissitudes this is a lovely pond. In autumn it has one more thing going for it. When the teal first arrive they can be a little bit naive and, even when fired upon, only fly as far as a small pond just two fields away. At this time of year this second pond, being located in a substantial hollow, is easily walked up so that there is usually a second bite of the cake on offer.

For some of the more open ponds, walking up may have to become crawling up if one is to get a shot. In the burning enthusiasm of youth this was never a problem and it did not even matter if the ground was wet and muddy. But for those of us of more mature years there is a very definite temptation to pass. Once the joints begin to creak it is bad enough having to indulge in a long crawl without then having to stand up quickly and swing one's gun sweetly. There will be times under such circumstances when the only hope of bagging a duck is to shoot it on the water. Some see this as fair sport, as considerable fieldcraft had to be exercised in order to get into position for a shot. They are perfectly entitled to their view and I have no problem with it. However, as far as I am concerned, the only fair duck is a duck on the wing.

Combined walking up and driving

Some ponds lend themselves to a combination of walking up and driving. This dual approach can sometimes be gainfully employed in the case of those awkward ponds for which it is difficult but not quite impossible to make an approach. Safety must always be the paramount consideration as the walking and standing guns are likely to be quite close to each other. The simplest thing is to have a very definite rule that no shot is to be fired until the birds are the better part of a gunshot up. And it must be realised that if there are any trees in the vicinity, ricochet can occur in the most unlikely ways.

Once, whilst woodcock shooting, I learned a lesson about ricochet which I have never forgotten. A friend and I were walking on either side of a very high ash ditch which had a good base of brambles and other shrubs. A woodcock was flushed from the centre of the ditch and, having no other option, flew literally straight up. I allowed it to rise some sixty feet before firing. Despite this precaution a roar from the other side of the ditch indicated that I had managed to hit my friend. A single pellet had deflected almost straight downwards and struck him on the point of the jaw with quite considerable force. He likened the experience to receiving a full bloodied blow on the jaw.

When walking up, as with all kinds of shooting, you must take into account the prevailing wind. Duck invariably rise into the wind, but if it is strong and gusty they often attempt to swing back or to the side and use it to make good their escape.

When attempting to drive duck from a pond it is vital to take account of the wind. They will always rise into the wind but if it is at all strong and gusty they often attempt to swing back or to the side and use it to make good their escape.

Not far from here is a small deep pond which is ideal for this dual approach. It lies almost in the middle of a field with the nearest ditch about eighty yards away. The pond has a tiny island which supports three tall trees and is surrounded by ashes and elders. Being fairly secluded it is much favoured by teal for roosting. There are always some there, maybe only two or three one day but a dozen or two the next. Until the leaves have gone they always fly straight up when disturbed so everyone gets a shot. But later in the winter they become quite expert at exploiting alternative escape routes. They are quite likely to break out between the bare ash limbs. As a result there is need to exercise great caution as they can, on occasions, suddenly appear dangerously low.

Mallard and teal, it will be apparent, bear the brunt of walked up duck shooting. They do so because, as well as being very numerous, they are the least conservative of their kind when it comes to the question of habitat selection. Wigeon will be encountered on ponds on occasions but in my experience infrequently and then usually on fairly large, more open ones. Shoveler will use ponds but their distribution is patchy in most places and it is really a matter of luck if one comes across them. As to gadwall and pintail, I have never flushed the former from a pond. This however may be simply because their numbers are low in the areas in which I do most of my shooting. My impression of them is that, like wigeon, they are much more at home on broad stretches of open water. I have only once in my life encountered a pintail on a pond. They are essentially birds of sandy estuaries and flooded water meadows. My sole meeting was at a relatively small flight pond which we had only dug out the previous year. On the last morning of the year I walked down to this pond to feed it shortly after dawn. There were good numbers of mallard using the pond and we had friends coming for a shoot the following evening. It was a grey morning and whilst I was still some distance away, a single bird, which I initially assumed to be a mallard, rose from the bank. Then, for an instance, I thought I got a glimpse of a chocolate head. It was difficult to be certain in the poor light and it was flying low towards a clump of trees. Somehow I knew it was a pintail but could not be certain.

The next evening we were in position in good time for evening flight. Four guns went down to that particular pond whilst my two sons waited at another one further up the bog. They got no shooting at all but a succession of volleys from the new pond told them that we were in business. Eleven ducks were shot, ten mallard, and yes, a pintail. It was an adult male in full plumage and is presently undergoing the full treatment from a taxidermist in Kilkenny. We now live in hope that some more of these lovely ducks will visit our ponds next season.

Diving ducks, which inland essentially means pochard and tufted (*see opposite page*), do not lend themselves to walked up shooting. This because of their mode of getting airborne. There is little sport in shooting a bird

that is pattering across the surface in a laboured take-off run. A little reminiscent of the flapper shooting of earlier eras. However, once they are in the air it is a different matter entirely and on occasions it is possible to orchestrate a drive. Tufted duck in particular can be quite amenable to being driven. They will usually take a straight line away from the walking guns and are much less inclined than teal and mallard to break away to the sides.

CHAPTER NINE

FLIGHTING

Whilst there is no doubt that walking up ducks can have its moments, especially if the weather is severe, duck shooting is really all about flighting. Essentially this means lying in wait for them, mainly in the twilight hours, as they go about their business. Accepting that nothing is guaranteed in Nature, which is really a very good thing from the hunting perspective as the sport would lose a lot of its appeal if we could always anticipate the intentions of our quarry, ducks can be reasonably predictable during certain periods. In particular they are usually on the move around dawn and dusk. Unlike wild geese which generally prefer to do their feeding by day, ducks do most of their feeding at night, especially in areas in which they are hunted. In consequence they hit out from sanctuaries and other undisturbed watery places as the light fades and make for favoured feeding grounds.

Sometimes they will leave a few clues that they are visiting a certain spot. The man who knows his fowl will have spotted a few feathers washed into the edge or signs that pondweeds have been disturbed. And he will have spent the day in eager anticipation of the good things that may happen at dusk.

On other occasions the hunter will make for a certain place purely on 'spec' and for no better reason than that it is a place to which ducks traditionally go and where, in the past, he has enjoyed some modicum of success. Either way he will make sure that he is at the feeding grounds a little before dusk descends. Just a few minutes should be enough to decide the best position to lie in wait and, if necessary, to set up a hide.

The alternative to waiting at the feeding grounds is to lie in ambush at some point along the route between roosting and feeding grounds. On the coast, for example, it is possible to intercept ducks as they move inland in the fading light. A certain amount of luck may be necessary as they sometimes flight on a broad front rather than following a narrow and precise line. In these situations height can be a problem, especially if the ducks have received a baptism of fire. A little help from the elements in the form of a good stiff head wind is no bad thing on these occasions. Few things are more frustrating than sitting under a good flight of ducks, all of which are crossing a couple of gunshots above one's head.

In the early morning there are the same two options. Either the hunter can wait on the roosting grounds or he can select a likely ambush point on the flight line. One difficulty with this second option is that there are mornings when the ducks decide to move early, well before there is sufficient light to see them. On such occasions it may not be possible to determine the exact flight line until the flight is well advanced and the bulk of them have already headed out to sea. Many a time I have strained my eyes in the pre-dawn darkness for some slightest sighting of the wings that are whispering overhead. And many a time the wings passed on, invisible in the black sky.

US pass shooting and point shooting

In North America lying in ambush along a flight line is commonly referred to as 'pass shooting'. It may rely upon that regular movement between roosting and feeding grounds. But, when the great autumnal migration gets underway, the ambush may be sited at some traditional spot on the journey south. It could, for example, be a marsh or lake where the fowl touch down for a while. In *American Duck Shooting* George Bird Grinnell gives some magnificent accounts of pass shooting in the late 1800s in such places as New England and North Dakota. In those far-off days, the sheer numbers of ducks and geese on the move must have been a truly awe inspiring sight. Essentially pass shooting involves the taking of en-route birds overhead or crossing, as opposed to the method of lying in wait for incoming birds referred to in the States as 'point shooting'. Essentially it is the same as the European lying in wait at the feeding or roosting grounds. But since there is no shooting during the hours of darkness in North America it differs in that it is a daytime activity. On both sides of the Atlantic a hide, or blind as it is called in North America, is sometimes used. Or the hunter may simply make use of whatever cover Nature provides in the immediate area. In point shooting, the ducks may take one or more precautionary circuits or, if they are newly arrived immigrants ill-educated in the ways of man, they may just come straight in.

Dawn or dusk?

For any given area, a number of factors will combine to determine whether morning or evening is the optimum time for flighting.

Young mallard enjoying their morning 'fix' of barley.

Amongst these are the size of the shooting territory, the local water regime and the location of sanctuaries/reserves. Should water be scarce in the area, best results are likely to be obtained by evening flighting. The ducks can be attracted, if necessary, by regular feeding. Evening flighting is also likely to be the best proposition in places where water meadows flood but do not retain water for too long. On the other hand, the presence of a lake or other large and fairly permanent water body may indicate suitability for shooting returning birds at dawn. Whatever option is best suited to a particular shooting territory, one matter is paramount. A sufficiently long period must be left between shoots to allow shattered avian nerves a chance to recover.

Other rather more mundane factors may also influence the choice between morning and evening flighting. For many, the demands of home and workplace often rule out early morning forays. These may be OK in early September when morning flight is likely to begin soon after 5am so that one can be safely home before the world has really woken up. But by October, the nights are lengthening and, in the modern idiom, the window of opportunity is slowly and steadily closing. Allowing for such variables as rain and cloud cover, I work on the basis that morning flight,

A party of flighters and their dogs assembles after a successful evening.

on average, comes two minutes later each passing day. And, of course, evening flight moves forward by the same two minutes.

In addition to dawn and dusk there are certain other occasions, some rather less predictable, when ducks can be flighted. I have referred, for example, to the great migratory flights moving south in North America which can be intercepted during the hours of daylight. In Britain and Ireland the period running up to and immediately following the full moon can be a productive one for dedicated duck hunters. Because, presumably, the dusk never fully descends at this time of the month, ducks tend to become restless and can be on the move all night long. This can be an exhilarating form of shooting, as the landscape, whether salt marsh or flooded water meadow, becomes a new and very different world when moonlit. During these hours of partial darkness, ducks, and wigeon in particular, tend to travel around their favourite feeding grounds. The wild geese too, which normally spend their nights on lochs or coastal sandbars, feed on into the small hours rather than returning to their roosts at dusk. Moon flighting is less predictable than evening flighting in that one can never be quite sure when ducks will take to the wing. It may be an hour or so after sunset or it may be a few hours. When the moon is high in the sky at the time of evening when darkness would otherwise descend, there may be little movement of fowl initially. Just the odd few teal or mallard may give way to hunger and put in a premature appearance.

Moon flighting really demands a fairly large wetland area so that there is the possibility of fowl moving on and off over a number of hours. Waiting by a small pond is not a good idea. Maybe a couple of mallard will oblige within a reasonable timespan but, equally, with the perversity of their kind they may well delay their visit for several hours.

Less predictable even than moon flighting is flighting a large loch or salt marsh during the hours of daylight. This may be done from a point of concealment on the bank, from an island or from a boat well hidden in some convenient reed bed. During periods of stormy weather, ducks that would usually spend their days roosting and preening well out on the water are apt to fly in search of less turbulent spots. Sheltered bays and river outlets can, on these sort of occasions, deliver the goods. If one is lucky to hit upon the right vantage point, it is possible to get some first class shooting. For reasons that I cannot really explain, diving ducks in particular have a habit of keeping on the move during stormy weather. Under these circumstances they can provide every manner of shot as they zip to and fro in the wind. Similar movements of ducks can also develop on broad rivers and estuaries when the weather turns wild.

Hides and concealment

The importance of concealment cannot be stressed enough. Whilst from time to time one may encounter ducks clearly displaying suicidal tendencies, which come into range when one is out in the open, the human form is generally guaranteed to keep them well out of gunshot. It is mainly naive young birds and recently-arrived migrants that pay the price for adopting an over-trusting attitude to mankind.

My personal preference is to find a place of concealment rather than constructing some sort of hide. This is undoubtedly to do with laziness. Some people enjoy the convenience of an instant hide made from a few alloy poles and netting. So be it. I just cannot be bothered to hump the makings around with me. But it must be admitted that there are now some excellent lightweight hides on the market. Depending upon circumstances, I prefer to seek the shelter of a broken breakwater, muddy creek, reeds or the like.

Just once in a while my cover has provided more than I bargained for. A case in point was on an October morning a few years back. I discovered that a considerate farmer had set a field of maize right up to the edge of a broad channel just behind the sea wall. I was delighted with the cover that the crop provided as it was well over six feet in height. Then, settling in, with dawn still a few minutes away, I became aware of strange rustling and gnawing noises. It was not until the first streaks of daylight appeared that I realised that I was not alone in my 'hide'. Literally thousands of rats were busily climbing the maize stems and feasting on the cobs. Despite this inconvenience a great flight developed and I shot a fine bag of teal and pintail.

In more rugged times dedicated fowlers went to extraordinary lengths to conceal themselves in the most barren of places. I once knew a man who had succeeded in burying a large beer barrel way out on mudflats.

Some people enjoy the convenience of an instant hide made from a few alloy poles and netting. I prefer to seek the shelter of a broken breakwater, muddy creek, reeds or the like.

He was able to seal it against the tide with a well-fitting lid and a washer he had made from an old motorcycle tyre. It stayed reasonably dry during high water and gave him a superb (but rather uncomfortable) vantage point when ducks and geese were on the wing. I tried it once – but never again. Maybe some human bodies are so sculptured that they fit comfortably into a barrel, so comfortably in fact that they can swing a shotgun with reasonable ease. My body is not so sculptured.

Clothing and camouflage

About clothing, little need be said. Common sense dictates that it should be such as to allow the wearer to blend in with his surroundings. This is especially important when morning light is coming and when one is flighting under the moon. All manner of magnificent camouflage gear is now available, some with matching guns for the more fashion-conscious of fowlers. I am not fully convinced of the necessity to go to such lengths. As long as one is clothed in muted shades of brown/olive/green, this normally suffices. Some sort of head-gear is vital. My preference is for an ordinary flat cap. I dislike the balaclava-type head-gear for two reasons. Most importantly, I want to hear the birds coming. Anything which covers or partly covers the ears reduces one's capacity to pick up that distant murmuring of wings or the far-off call of fowl. Secondly I find it plain uncomfortable to have my head swathed in any form of garment.

Wild duck vision

All birds have phenomenal vision. Wildfowl are no exceptions. An interesting comparison between the visual acuity of a kestrel and a human was published some years ago. The comparison, I believe, holds true for birds generally. It was made by reference to the size of an object on the ground that could be detected from a height of one hundred feet above it. The kestrel can detect something of the size of a black beetle, ie rather less than an inch in length. Poor mankind can just about make out something the size of a rat – and that is if he has 20/20 vision. Not surprisingly therefore, an incoming duck will quickly adjust its flight path in response to the slightest hint of lurking humanity. The two big clues that indicate that all is not well below (from the duck's point of view, that is) are movement, even the very slightest, and the whiteness of an exposed face. Hardier men of former eras remedied this latter by the liberal application of mud. Modern man, brought up on a diet of television advertising which raises serious questions about his masculinity if he does not apply liberal quantities of body sprays/gels to his person, might forego the mud treatment. For him, therefore, the netting face mask.

When fowl are circling, there is a terrible temptation to look up too soon. This must be avoided at all costs. One must learn to trust one's ears and respond to the various aural clues that flighting ducks provide: the magical whispering of wings growing ever-louder, the increasingly noisy chatter of incoming mallard, the whistling of wigeon cocks intensifying when they are satisfied that all is well below. For wild geese coming into decoys, especially pinkfeet, the tell-tale sounds are even more pronounced. Having circled a few times, their clamour suddenly goes up a number of decibels when, finally, they are satisfied to make their landing run.

Decoys

Long before the invention of firearms, mankind was using models of ducks to lure the genuine articles into positions where they could be netted, shot with bow and arrow or otherwise be captured. Native Americans were using their own decoys (as opposed to the duck decoys that originated in Holland) for centuries before the coming of Europeans. The first of them were made from reeds, clearly an aid to buoyancy, and the earliest that have been discovered are no mean replicas of canvasbacks. With the development of increasingly efficient shotguns and a parallel expansion of commercial hunting, decoys quickly became essential items of the duck hunter's equipment. They have always been very much part of the wildfowl hunting tradition of North America.

In Europe their use, though widespread, is to a large extent a matter of personal preference. In North America the sheer size of many of the

Collecting up decoys after the flight.

duck shooting territories is such as to necessitate any available means of drawing fowl into range, especially so in a shooting regime which centres upon the hours of daylight. In contrast, for many Europeans, our sport revolves around evening flight over ponds or winter splashes. It is often a question in such places of whether or not the ducks will come at all. In consequence, decoys do not always figure in our scheme of things. This being said, if the water area is fairly large, there is no question but that properly sited decoys can deliver. Then again, we have all experienced evenings on which ducks have studiously ignored them.

For generations, decoys were carved from wood. Many were, and indeed remain, magnificent examples of the carver's skill and they command high prices as collectors' items. Rubber decoys eventually replaced them and these in turn gave way to ones made from synthetic materials. I started with the rubber articles many years ago. It was not an auspicious start. My first purchase had been of half a dozen of what in charity might be described as mallard decoys. They looked clumsy, they were clumsy, but they were roughly mallard-shaped and mallard-

Invariably I would choose one pond – and the duck, in truly unsporting manner, would opt for a different one.

coloured. The biggest plus was that they floated reasonably well.

In those days I had the shooting of a cousin's bog almost to myself, or so I thought, as there were few people shooting in the area and those that did were only interested in pheasants. I had acquired my decoys in time for 1st September and with the naivety of youth was convinced that they would provide me with a mighty bag on that opening evening. The bog in question is well over a mile in length and is bisected by a stream which opens into smallish ponds at a number of points. My problem in previous seasons had always been that of selecting the correct one of these for evening flight. There was always a good number of duck in the bog but almost invariably I would choose one pond and they, in truly unsporting manner, would opt for a different one.

On that fateful evening in early September my decoys were in position and I was securely concealed in a nearby ditch well before the appointed hour. One great thing about this particular bog from the shooting viewpoint is that, for most of its length, a hefty ditch runs parallel to the stream, in most places not more than thirty or forty yards from it. I was enjoying the last of the day's sunshine and watching swallows skimming over the water when two rapid shotgun blasts in close proximity caused me to nearly jump out of my skin.

The surface of the pond positively boiled in a hail of lead and then, when the shock-waves began to abate, I saw my decoys like so many drunken men listing at every conceivable angle. Because of the tight-knit nature of the ditch, I had to travel the best part of a hundred yards to find a gap into the field from which the shots had been fired. By this time the decoy assassin was beating a hasty retreat across the far side of the field. He had obviously quickly realised the enormity of his crime and had decided that discretion was the better part of valour.

After that particular episode, I did not use my decoys again for quite a long time. Of my original six, two were beyond repair and three more, though still capable of floating, were well and truly peppered above the water line.

Very many years later I had another unhappy experience with decoys, this time in very different surroundings. On the occasion in question I was treated to a demonstration of just how efficient they can be given the right circumstances. This sounds like something of a contradiction so I must explain. At the time I was a regular attender at a large commercial duck shoot. The central part of the shoot, which extended over several thousand acres, consisted of a broad estuary. Along the banks, which in places were between 2–300 yards apart were hides, some set in reed beds. The shoot was adjacent to the sea so that in addition to the released mallard, there was often an assortment of migratory ducks on the move. On that fateful morning I had drawn a hide which was situated diagonally across from one which housed one of the shoot's guides plus, it transpired, two companions. This was, in retrospect, a quite extraordinary state of affairs considering that the same gentleman's job was supposed to be looking after the guns in his care. Anyway the sporting trio had the better part of a hundred decoys floating in front of their hide. A good flight developed just after dawn. Across from me, the said sporting trio could not go wrong…. their raft of decoys had a magnetic effect on the ducks and their bag steadily mounted. I suppose that this was very much a situation made for decoying. Having been fed regularly for a couple of weeks, the normal interval between shoots, the ducks were unwilling to vacate the area despite the ongoing barrage of shots. Presumably they saw the great assembly of decoys as a place of sanctuary. For the record, nothing came near me. My couple of ultra long-range shots failed to down a bird that morning, something, it should be said, that did little for what I like to think of as my normal, sunny disposition.

Today, hanging side by side in an outhouse on our farm are two large grey canvas bags bulging with decoys. If the bags were opened I have no doubt that they would reveal, in addition to the decoys, an unholy tangle of nylon lines attached to an assortment of large nuts, bolts, old spanners and other less identifiable pieces of steel. Despite my passion for duck shooting, these decoys rarely see the light of day. There are two reasons for this.

The first relates to the sorts of places in which I do most of my duck shooting: marshy ponds, bogs, small rivers and the like where, as intimated earlier, decoys confer no real advantage. Even when the winter floods come to our valley the stretches of water rarely amount to much more than a couple of acres.

My second reason for being a touch ambivalent about decoys has to do with dogs. Some people own dogs that retrieve their decoys for them. I have never owned a dog that had the slightest interest in so doing. I have never really made up my mind as to whether they were all simply thick and incapable of understanding this part of their job description or were too bright to be fooled by these impostors. To compound matters I have had occasions when a duck was dropped into the decoy pattern and the dog succeeded in getting tangled in the anchoring lines. Typical scenario – dog furiously treading water and howling, me hoping it will free itself and thus absolve me of the necessity of getting very cold and very wet extracting it.

DECOY LAYOUT ON A FLOODED WATER MEADOW

Decoys should be well spaced and mainly in an area extending from 20-30 yards from the hide. My preference is for an 'empty' killing zone within the decoy arrangement.
As the duck frequently engage in a few precautionary circuits they are likely to fly over the hide, so it is important that it has a good, well-camouflaged back.

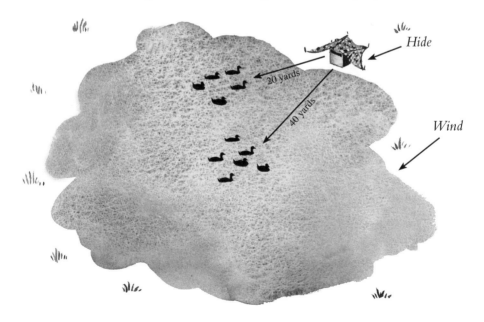

Whatever about the aforementioned ambivalence in relation to decoys for duck shooting, I am fully convinced of the need to use them for inland goose shooting over stubbles or grass. Pinkfeet and greylags decide upon a particular field, usually a large one, and continue to visit each morning as long as there is no disturbance and there is food available. The only hope of coming to terms with them is to weave long strands of grass into the almost inevitable barbed wire boundary fence, set up a net to provide a modicum of concealment and then put out a lot, and I mean a lot, of decoys. We have used up to two hundred on occasions. I am sure that the same holds true in North America where the vastness of the stubbles means that without decoys there would be little or no chance of getting in range of geese. Watching film of stubble flighting there, I am always intrigued by the mixture of Canada geese and mallard which frequent the same stubble ground. In all my years of shooting geese over Scottish stubbles I have rarely seen more than the very odd mallard in the air even though, in some areas, there is no shortage of them.

Here in west Tipperary we are fortunate to enjoy some very good stubble flighting in September, especially during the early part of the month. From time to time I have used decoys in this situation but have never found them to be of much value. Admittedly though, I have never put out more than a couple of dozen. Whether it be at dawn and dusk, the mallard have a habit of visiting twice a day, they seem to know exactly the part of the field they want and the decoys simply do not cause them to change their collective mind. It may be that my flat bottomed specimens are not sufficiently conspicuous in stubbles, especially if they are on the high side. Perhaps if I were to use larger-than-life decoys I might fare better.

Large decoys

I must now be very honest. I had always treated extra large decoys with more than a little derision. Film of sheep-sized Canada goose decoys, for example, set up in massed ranks, struck me as being particularly ludicrous. Until last October that is. It was the final morning of an exceptionally good week's goose shooting in eastern Scotland. As usual we were busily engaged setting up a great assembly of decoys in that special darkness

Gathering up the large goose decoys – the exaggerated scale did not seem to concern the incoming birds one iota.

that precedes the dawn and hoping that the geese would oblige one final time. Expectations were heightened when the first hint of light revealed a lot of greenish droppings and grey brown feathers in the stubbles. But then, consternation. In the half light a landrover towing a double horse box drove into an adjoining field. This field lay between us and a not too distant loch on which several thousand pinkfeet were roosting. As the day brightened we could only sit and watch as a positive horde of the biggest decoys that we had ever seen were put out.

Usually in late October the grey geese leave their nocturnal roosts and head for stubble ground somewhere between 8am and 9am, on an average morning nearer to the latter hour. On the morning in question, as is sometimes their wont, they moved rather later than usual. Sometime after 10am there were serious numbers of pinkfeet in the sky, skein after skein, all heading in our direction. But, despite our small army of decoys not so much as a single goose reached our field. Those enormous decoys in the next field bewitched every one of them. In this deception they were aided and abetted by electronic calls which, we later discovered, were being operated by three 'sportsmen' from southern Europe. These gentlemen were equipped with semi automatic shotguns and they took a mighty toll from each skein. Indeed so fast were they shooting that we suspected that they were simply discharging their guns into the massed ranks as they swept in. Needless to say we were rather less than happy campers.

Any lingering doubts that I might have harboured about the efficacy of jumbo-sized goose decoys were quickly put to rest this year. Our guide had acquired a few dozen of them and they unquestionably delivered the goods. The weather was windy throughout our stay in Scotland and this resulted in the geese flying lower than usual. I think that this windy weather really helped the big decoys to come into their own. The geese were able to see them at a distance despite their lower trajectories, something they could not have done with conventional decoys.

What to look for in a decoy

When buying decoys a number of things need to be borne in mind. Shape, and specifically the position of the head, is all-important. Ducks roosting out on open water relax their neck muscles allowing their heads to lie low on their bodies. This is the stance that should be replicated in order to set at ease the minds of birds passing in the vicinity. A straight neck with head held high usually suggests a duck that is not fully at ease. This being said, there is no harm in having in one's decoy flock the odd one with head up. In any flock of wild birds, be they roosting or feeding, there will always be a few on the alert.

Then there is the question of colour. Nothing is more guaranteed to send fowl flaring to the clouds than garish decoys glinting in the sun. Always go for sombre specimens. Personally I prefer a big majority of females as their dowdy colours are less likely to reflect light and set alarm bells ringing. I suspect that in most lights it is the silhouettes that initially arouse the interest of passing birds.

Much has been written about setting out a decoy pattern but I am far from convinced that there is anything approaching rocket science involved. A pack of ducks on the water will, inevitably, assume something of a random distribution. All that can be said is that the majority will, at any one time, be facing into the wind and that there will be irregular spacing between individuals. Getting one's decoys to face into the wind is not a problem. To state perhaps the obvious, as long as they are attached by their front ends to a submerged weight they have little option but to take up the desired position.

If one watches incoming ducks joining their colleagues on the water they will be seen to do one of two things. Either they will pitch into a space between birds, providing that there is a reasonable sufficiency of free water, or, more commonly, they will alight at the fringes of the pack. In this latter case they will, in the main, opt for the fringes farthest away from any cover. Consequently, when setting out decoys, the nearest to one's point of concealment should be reasonably close, certainly not much more than twenty yards. The farthest should be between thirty and forty yards away. After this the precise disposition of the pattern is largely a matter of personal preference. I suspect that throwing them out at random is as good a method as any. For geese on stubbles we always leave an empty 'killing zone' in the middle of the pattern. This means, effectively, that the decoys are in two groups and the central killing zone is straight out from where we are concealed. On the rare occasions in recent years when I have used decoys for ducks I have adopted this strategy and found it to work satisfactorily.

Duck-calling

My views on the use of calls to lure birds into range are simplistic in the extreme. I refer specifically to the ones that are blown as opposed to the electronic variety. If you have a good ear you are likely to use them to good effect. My youngest son is so blessed. But, if like me you have a brutal ear, leave them in the safe hands of others better endowed in this respect. There is nothing better guaranteed to send ducks and geese into the next parish than a call that is slightly, or maybe not so slightly, different from their own. For hard of hearing incompetents such as myself I would make one exception. The simple disc-shaped wigeon call that fits between the front teeth and the lips is a sure fire winner for the simple reason that it seems to produce only the correct sound. Be warned though, whilst it can also be used to imitate the piping of teal, this does demand a greater degree of competency.

To watch a master caller in action is a treat indeed. In the case of geese distant specks whose clamour is just about audible can be drawn magnetically to the decoys by his artistry. It is an art in which I would love to be proficient but know that I never will be. Mind you, it is very hard work, especially if one is attempting to call in geese that are a bit decoy-shy. I have seen strong men in need of a serious respite after a prolonged conversation with suspicious geese.

Electronic calls, essentially amplified recordings of the real thing, are readily available but in my estimation have no place in the hunting field. What is more their use for quarry species (as opposed to predatory ones) is quite correctly illegal in most countries. The manufacturers of the ones that I have come across give their product a semi-legitimacy by incorporating the calls of a number of pest and wildfowl species onto the same tape or disk. A few years ago I was invited to an evening duck flight in late December. The venue was a very long specially dug out pond adjacent to a small river. As dusk fell the air in the place began to resonate with the excited piping of incoming teal. But try as I might, not a teal could I see in the darkening sky. Then I realised that one of the guns at the opposite end of the pond was playing one of these devices at maximum amplification. It certainly brought in the teal. To him. The man in question got seven or eight and his immediate neighbours benefited as well. Needless to say not a single teal came to my end of the pond.

Dogs: essential for wildfowling

Finally there is the dog, an essential companion whenever one is flighting ducks. Indeed, if for no other reason than a wounded bird should never be left behind, no one should even contemplate a fowling trip without a canine assistant. What is required, essentially, is a strong, big hearted dog which will not baulk at being sent into cold or fast flowing water time and time again. Labradors and golden retrievers fit the bill extremely well. Some swear by the curly coated Irish Water Spaniel but this is a breed about which I have certain reservations. They are undoubtedly great water dogs but I have seen them miss wounded birds that were later picked up by other dogs. As well as this I am not fully convinced of their staying power when they are required to work in very cold or very rough water.

My invariable companion is a springer spaniel. We do a lot of woodcock shooting as well as duck shooting and these big-hearted bundles of energy serve us admirably in both capacities. Down the years it has been my privilege to own some superb springers, dogs totally devoid of fear even in the face of the most tempestuous of conditions. Admittedly the white part of their coats is not the best when it comes to concealment but they are small dogs and can usually be hidden in a clump of reeds or other vegetation. Few dogs, in my experience, cope better with a wounded duck which is diving, resurfacing and diving again. A good springer quickly learns to bide its time and tread water until the moment presents at which it can make the capture.

Springers are my first choice as gundogs. They seem completely devoid of fear and have a great ability to find and retrieve wounded duck from the water.

Ducks can be flighted at dawn and at dusk and under the moon. They can be flighted over stubbles. Each of these has its own special flavour and is dealt with separately in the following chapters.

CHAPTER TEN

FLIGHTING AT DAWN

A lot of people are up and about in time to see the coming of dawn during the winter months. But few seem to have the inclination to watch and to listen to the breathtaking events that surround the beginning of each new day. In fairness, I suppose, most of them nowadays live in places where few wild creatures live and where, anyway, the continuous roar of traffic drowns out what sounds there are of the natural world. And then there are the endless rows of yellow orange sodium vapour lights which mute the colours of the brightening sky. As for the good people themselves, many are fully occupied attending to the numerous calls of the material world. All important, they must go to work, the greatest curse of the human race. I was forcibly reminded of this whilst on a short trip to Germany some years ago.

We were staying in the town of Kleve which is just a few miles away from the Dutch border. It is a delightful place linked to the mighty Rhine by the Spoykanel. During autumn and winter the area plays host to countless grey geese. An hour or so after dawn the sky is positively alive with white-fronts and greylags going about their daily business. It was our habit whilst staying in Kleve to have dinner in the hotel around 7.30pm and then, an hour or so later, to take a stroll around the town. There was one thing we could not understand when we took those evening walks. Soon after 9pm the streets would be all but deserted so that we had the town almost to ourselves.

However all was made clear on our final morning there. We were booked back on an early flight from Dusseldorf and this necessitated leaving the hotel at 4.15am. Emerging from the hotel at this early hour, an hour indeed at which 99% of the folk back home would still be slumbering peacefully, we were surrounded by a great bustle of activity. At least half of the population of Kleve, or so it seemed, was already on the way to work. The train to Dusseldorf was packed. No one, just no one, had a moment to spare to stop or look or listen. No wonder they all went to bed so early.

To really appreciate the dawn in all its majesty one needs time. Time

A pair of teal – the sound of their arrival in the stillness of dawn never fails to raise the waiting fowler's pulse.

to see and watch and listen. This is something that the fowler shares with ancestors of very long ago. To those ancient peoples it was surely a time of great reassurance. Every day of their lives they saw a world of darkness, shrouded in all the primeval fears of humankind, translated into one of light and hope. And it is that latter word, hope, that epitomises the mindset of the fowler as he sits and waits for the events of the new day to unfold. A rather different sort of hope, but hope nevertheless. His hope is all about mallard and wigeon, pintail and teal. It is a hope that they will come aplenty. And not only come, but come neither too high nor too wide.

In that darkness before the first faint hint of light enters the sky the familiar sounds of wild wet places are all around one. Locality and time of year together dictate the precise combinations of these sounds. In coastal regions the crash of distant waves far out across the mud and the gurgle of the tide as creeks fill and empty are ever-present. Inland, on a balmy September morning, the 'plop' of a greedy trout may be the only sound to break the stillness of the dawn air. But come December, with the blast of a south westerly cutting across the bog, there will be the singing of the reed beds, the lapping of water as it is hurled against the banks and the creak of ancient willows as they submit to the ferocity of the wind.

Then there are the calls of the denizens of the wetlands, both web-footed and hen-footed. Some of these birds cannot wait for the coming of the light to go about their business. Whether by the sea or inland the emotive 'coor-li' of the curlew is all but guaranteed to come floating down the wind. Once winter is really with us the 'whee-oo' of the wigeon cocks is a sound that never fails to raise the waiting fowler's pulse. And then there are the pinkfeet and other geese. The great majority of them will not think of taking to the air until the sun has broken the horizon. But out on the sand bars their clamour grows. There will be though, surely, at least one small and restless skein that insists upon an early departure for the feeding grounds. Unseen in the darkness only a distant 'wink wink' betrays their passing.

As well as by their calls, some wildfowl identify themselves by the sounds of their flight. One moment there is the bell-like music of mute swans on the wing, the next a rush of displaced air as a pack of teal or golden plovers whistle by no more than feet above the mud. Usually not too far from the sea that strange humming sound of flighting goldeneye gives warning that the main movement of ducks will not be too long delayed. Often as not the first flights will pass over well in range but safe in the all-pervading darkness.

But early as some fowl move there is, inland, one bird that beats them all. It is the woodcock, the wader that has deserted its ancestral haunts for the security of scrub and forest. Just once in a while you will hear it pass, long before the coming of the light. At dusk the previous evening it set out for marshy feeding grounds, usually not too far from its woodland home, and then spent the hours of darkness probing for worms after the manner of its kind. Then, appetite sated, it makes for home in total darkness. Occasionally, driving along a forest road before dawn (for perfectly legitimate reasons let me add), one picks up a woodcock in the headlights just standing on the road. This is their way. They flight into a road or other open space and then, at their leisure, simply stroll into cover. In my experience they do not travel far from that point of touchdown. When shooting woodcock in a forest, one is always more likely to spring them near the edge of a track or clearing than from deep amongst the trees.

Ideal dawn shooting conditions

Dawn can arrive in a variety of moods; cold and icy still, wild and wet, balmy but with threatening black clouds building steadily. And these moods will affect the fowl in different ways. Some will prompt an early start to the proceedings of the day, others will cause them to sit tight until the day has all-but arrived. If the duck hunter could select conditions for his foray, his choice would not be too difficult. Number one on the agenda would be a good brisk wind. This would help to ensure that the birds, or at least a good proportion of them, would not cross many gunshots up. What do I mean precisely by a gunshot? In the context of duck shooting, especially in coastal parts, 40 yards or maybe a little more.

Modern cartridges, in contrast to the paper-cased versions of my youth, can do extraordinary things so maybe, just maybe, I am erring a little on the conservative side. Just two seasons ago I learned a salutary lesson about the power of the modern cartridge. We were flighting, or more precisely going through the motions of flighting, geese over stubbles. There were plenty of pinkfeet around but for some inexplicable reason they were fighting shy of our decoys. In less than an hour many hundreds had come, seen and decided to depart. Then a party of three greylags swept across high and embarked upon a landing run, only to break away at the last minute. They were a long way out and I should not have fired. No excuse perhaps but frustration took over and I fired the choke barrel which was loaded with a three inch cartridge containing nearly two ounces of BB. One goose fell dead. A second dropped a few yards further out and was safely retrieved by a colleague. In total disbelief he paced the distance back to our hide. It was just short of 90 yards. Let me quickly add that I do not advocate shooting at this range.

So a good wind yes, but not a violent one. Storm force winds will certainly bring birds down from the clouds. But the downside is that it is nearly impossible to swing a gun smoothly when both it and oneself are being subjected to a severe buffeting. As well as this, the ducks are being

One goose fell dead. A second dropped a few yards further out and was safely retrieved by a colleague.

tossed around in the sky making them difficult targets. Teal in particular can be next to impossible in these conditions.

Wind, unfortunately for those of us living close to the Atlantic, all too often comes coupled with a heavy dose of rain. Rarely, in my experience, does one get a decent flight at dawn if there is continuous heavy rain. Squally showers are one thing and do not usually detract too much from the business in hand, but a prolonged shower in the twilight hour both delays and disrupts the morning flight. I do not think that I have ever shot more than a half-decent bag of ducks when it was very wet at dawn.

So far then, for the ideal flight: a moderate-to-strong wind and no rain. Two other factors need to be considered: the stage of the moon and, for those shooting the saltings, the stage of the tide. In a previous chapter I mentioned that ducks and geese change their habits around the time of the full moon. They can be on the move on and off throughout the night and ducks may well have returned to their daytime roosts well before dawn. Morning flight can thus become something of a hit and miss affair. For our ideal flight, in consequence, we would select the blackest period between the moons. As to the tide, we would like it full, coming up to dawn. With a good brisk wind stirring up the sea, roosting conditions become rather less than comfortable and the ducks are inclined to stay longer on the wing than usual.

There can be quite considerable variation in both the time at which flight starts and its duration. On occasions it can get underway early and be nearly over before the light has fully come. One such flight will remain long in my mind. It took place on a shoot next to the sea which I attended for many years. Near the centre of the shoot, a wide channel ran up to the sea wall. Two hides were strategically situated at the end of this channel and nestled under the sea wall. On a shooting morning, a time was agreed for the start of shooting which gave everyone adequate time to reach their hides. Some of them were accessible from farm roads, others required quite a long walk. Ideally, the appointed time was such as to allow everyone to reach their hides well before the ducks began to stir. What made this shoot special was that the ducks would flight both out to sea and in from the sea as the light came. Some days they could be on the move for several hours after dawn. Incoming birds were attracted by the generous helpings of barley sweepings deposited at strategic locations. They also took advantage of the shelter of dense reed beds when the sea was in an ugly mood.

On the morning in question I had drawn my favourite hide. It was one of the two under the sea wall and was in line with the centre of the channel. This location usually ensured that one was under the main flight line or very near to it. In those days, ducks of many species were wont to fly back and forth and, by mid winter, sea-loving ducks such as scaup and goldeneye were very much in evidence. That particular morning one of two things happened. Either there had been a slight miscalculation of the starting time or the light came a fraction early. Anyway, before the appointed hour and with the first and faintest hint of daybreak, a flight of ducks got underway the like of which one rarely sees. There was just enough wind to keep them down and for some ten to fifteen minutes, a

The best morning flights inland generally occur where there are broad expanses of floodwater.

positive stream of black silhouettes passed over me, almost all of them in fair range. The temptation to start shooting prematurely was mighty but I held my fire, consoling myself with the thought that good things were sure to continue after this auspicious start. But good things positively failed to happen.

By the time that shooting could start, the flight had dried up and for the rest of the morning there was only the odd bird on the move. I had been under one of the best flights that it had ever been my privilege to witness and I had not shot a single duck.

The story has a post script. Some years later a similar event occurred. This time I was some way back from the sea wall but near enough to see and hear what was happening. Again the scheduled kick off time was a little late. Again a magnificent flight took place. The difference was that the temporary residents of the sea wall were not going to miss as good a chance as this. Very early on, a veritable fusillade of shots began and lasted for a good half hour. In a memorable rugby match at Twickenham between England and Ireland, memorable at least from the Irish point of view, *The Times* next day described an Irish forward, one Ginger McLouglin, as crossing the line 'festooned with Sassenachs'. Our heroes from the sea wall could be described with similar poetic licence at the end of the shoot. They appeared festooned with ducks of every description.

Earlier this year I had a very different experience of morning flight at a shoot not very far from the one described above. It was late September and the first arrivals of wigeon and teal were much in evidence. Conditions for flighting were ideal. A fairly strong wind, gusting at times, was blowing from the south east and favouring my hide. The morning was grey so that dawn came slowly and, all important, except for a few flurries of rain, it remained dry. There was little on the move in the half light and it was quite a while before any shooting erupted. But then an extremely serious flight of ducks began to develop, mainly mallard but with a useful complement of wigeon and teal. Initially, such can be the perversity of the creatures of the wilds, my neighbouring gun got plenty of shooting. Despite the favourable wind the ducks decided to give me a wide berth.

Fortunately this sad state of affairs did not last for long. As the morning progressed, the wind strengthened and the ducks finally had little option but to come my way. They then continued to do so for nearly an hour. So plentiful were the mallard that we eventually decided to grant them safe passage and concentrated on the teal. No duck provides more challenging shooting when the weather turns wild. Whatever about the first bird, the second provides the ultimate challenge as it tears for the Heavens propelled by a combination of its own musculature and the forces of Nature.

Except when a large pond or lake is guarded jealously and shot sparingly, the best morning flights inland generally occur where there are broad expanses of floodwater. Under these conditions the ducks will have their preferred feeding and roosting areas which may change according to the depth of the water. As a general rule, the deeper and more secluded ones are used for roosting. If the feeding grounds provided by the flood-waters are near the coast, the ducks may well roost on the sea. In any event they will leave the feeding grounds at dawn and flight to the roosting waters.

Some of the best morning flights that I have experienced inland took place over the Ouse Washes north of Cambridge many years ago. Along the two banks of the river, and set fairly well back, are high flood walls protecting the surrounding land. But in those days, despite these barriers, countless acres of grassland were regularly submerged when the heavy rains came. Early in our student days we discovered this Mecca for wildfowl and spent rather more of our winters there than good, hard working students should have done. The floodwater was rarely very deep and a lot of it could be negotiated wearing waders. The field boundaries consisted of tall thorn hedges and for flight we would simply wade out and stand in against them. We never discovered in those carefree days who actually owned the land. And, despite many visits, we were never so much as challenged. Today, I strongly suspect, matters would be somewhat different.

Whilst the water remained in the fields, dawn was the time to be present. Later, when the floods had drained away, a few shallow pools in hollows provided some great evening flighting. Most of the ducks were wigeon. Mallard were never that plentiful but there was always a good scattering of pintail and teal. Inland, in those far distant days, dawn frequently came cold, crisp and clear rather than grey and wild. At daybreak, wigeon in their thousands would pass down heading mainly, I think, for the Bedford Levels. The majority of them would be high in the sky as befits such conditions. But there would usually be a few packs of careless ones to keep us gainfully employed. Teal would be on the move as well but they never appeared to be following a definite flight path. Like teal everywhere, they had that infuriating habit of zipping past low just when one was scanning the horizon in anticipation of another wigeon pack.

An unforgettable January dawn

There was one January morning on the Washes which none of us who were present will ever forget. It was one of the coldest mornings of my lifetime. Black ice had slowed our pre-dawn journey and the light was already coming when we reached the edge of the floodwaters. There was an icy and eerie stillness about the place. The water was frozen over but we were just about able to break our way through the ice as we made our way to our favourite positions for the flight. Not far from our destination, and about fifty yards from a hedge, we came across a mute swan frozen in the ice. Being kind-hearted people, we decided to free it. That was a mistake. The ungrateful creature literally went berserk when we approached it and repulsed our every effort with bill and wings. There was no option but to beat a strategic retreat. As we did so the swan somehow managed to free itself and proceeded to skitter off across the ice.

It was so cold that morning that the tracks that we made through the ice had already frozen over again before we reached our stands. By now it was quite light and there were wigeon on the move. They were mostly very high and only the odd one provided a shot. Numbed by a combination of the cold and lack of activity, I was standing in something of a trance when an enormous bang and a brilliant flash of orange returned me quickly to my senses. My nearest colleague's gun had exploded and he had fallen over on the ice. By great good fortune he was not injured though he later reckoned that it was some days before his hearing got back to normal, to say nothing of his nerves. What seemed to have happened was that whilst we were engaged in our mission of mercy with the swan, he had poked his barrels through the broken ice. The water that entered then promptly froze causing an obstruction. To this day I regularly check my barrels with almost excessive zeal as a result of that experience.

As a general rule, prolonged frost does little for morning flight. Duck numbers will certainly build up in coastal areas as inland waters freeze over but when they are on the move they usually seek the safety of high altitude. For the inland duck hunter, slow-flowing rivers provide the best hope for an early morning foray under such conditions. At and shortly after dawn, ducks tend to fly rather aimlessly up and down the river in search of suitable roosting quarters. This is the one situation in my experience in which decoys can be a positive asset at dawn. If one can get well out in a reed bed, or reach an island, there is always the chance of luring birds into range. Diving ducks, in particular tufties, I find decoy especially well during these periods of hard weather.

Here in Tipperary, our local river the Suir is, with one or two exceptions, too narrow to provide much of a dawn flight. Further downstream below Carrick where it draws nearer to the sea, it offers rather more promise. One of those few exceptions is, most fortuitously, not too distant from my home. It consists of a broad bend in the river where opposite banks are about 80 yards apart. Unless the river is in flood, the water here is quite shallow. Strangely, except during periods of prolonged frost, this stretch of the river holds little attraction for ducks. But during those freezing interludes, it really comes into its own. Probably because the sharp bend slows up the flow of water, it provides comfortable roosting quarters. In the immediate area there are a few farms with flooded water-meadows where shooting is not permitted.

Under normal circumstances some of these are used as roosts from which the ducks spread out to surrounding floodwaters each evening. But when everywhere around is frozen, many of the ducks wintering in the locality spend their days on the bend of the river. At dusk they flight out to small spring-fed ponds to feed. They return at dawn, or soon after it, often providing great shooting for about twenty minutes. Decoys are unnecessary as there is no alternative roost in the immediate area. If conditions are really severe, there is the possibility of a very mixed bag.

Teal are usually the first to return. They have an infuriating habit of flying low along the river and pitching in before one has time to raise the gun. The only answer is to flush them straightaway. Not quite the normal version of morning flight but great sport nevertheless. Then come the mallard. Most of them are residents, and having been exposed to shooting since 1st September, are understandably wary. They nearly always insist upon a number of precautionary circuits before making their landing run. These are the only circumstances under which we see pochard in this part of the valley. Shovelers come as well and just the occasional pintail. Shovelers in fact seem to be more common here during periods of hard frost. Last to arrive most mornings are the wigeon. I can think of no logical reason why this is the case but last they usually are. Very obligingly they tend to come in twos and threes and in small groups rather than the larger packs in which they usually travel.

Whilst this is a book about wild ducks and their hunters, no account of the magic of dawn would be complete without mention of those other majestic creatures, the wild geese, with which they share their lonesome

Shovelers seem to be more common in Tipperary during periods of hard frost.

and watery homes. In yet another of those many mysteries of Nature, the wild geese order their lives very differently to their closest relatives. For them it is a matter of feeding by day and roosting by night, even in places where the levels of shooting pressure are such as to suggest that it would be eminently sensible to reverse this schedule of events. Depending upon locality, the wild geese return at dusk to spend the hours of darkness on lochs, sand bars or winter flashes, sometimes surprisingly small ones. To a much lesser extent they may opt to spend the night on a slow-moving river. In the morning they set out for their feeding grounds which may be stubbles, grassy fields or, usually after the turn of the year, broad expanses of young winter corn.

Also unlike the wild ducks, which are anxious to be off to their feeding grounds as soon as dusk falls, at the other end of the day the wild geese are quite happy to wait until the light has fully come before setting forth. As the hour of lift-off approaches, the noise on the roost gradually intensifies until, with a roar of wings and much chatter, the first skeins are airborne. Sometimes they travel many miles to feed. This may be a corollary of heavy shooting pressure. If undisturbed, wild geese are likely to visit the same feeding grounds day after day until the food supply runs low.

In those areas fortunate enough to have both ducks and geese during the winter months, the events of the early morning are reasonably predictable. As we have seen, the ducks begin moving to the sea as the light comes. Most of them will have completed their journeys before the geese begin to move.

Occasionally an earlier than usual start for the geese may be prompted by a high and fast running tide pushing them off the sand bars. Should the duck hunter stay on, he will see the great skeins passing over. Once in a while the elements may favour him and force the geese to fly low. For the purist this is the perfect time and place to shoot wild geese as they swing ever higher over the mud. But conditions must be just right if he is to achieve his objective. On those few occasions on which I have visited the great goose grounds of the Solway, a cannon would have been necessary to bring down the pinkfeet, such was their height. In fairness though to the dedicated hunters who regularly shoot this wonderful estuary, my visits always seemed to coincide with periods of settled weather and brilliant blue skies.

Whilst the pinkfeet display a commendable reticence when it comes to having anything to do with mankind, the barnacle goose, a species which abounds on the Solway, has no such compunctions. This has, undoubtedly, a lot to do with its protected status. Even on the stillest of days they are quite likely to fly by in easy range, seemingly oblivious to one's presence. A similarly easy relationship exists between the other protected black goose, the Brent, and humanity. One of the most extraordinary sights is surely that of Brent geese grazing contentedly next to a busy road in a Dublin suburb, totally unfazed by the roar of passing traffic. Watching them only last week I was amused to see that one bunch hardly bothered to move when a couple of joggers passed within feet of them. And these, remember, are truly wild birds from the High Arctic which have crossed the Atlantic to spend the winter with us.

Nowadays most wild goose shooting in Britain – and this essentially means grey geese because the introduced Canada goose is the only black goose on the shooting list – takes place as they come into their feeding grounds. Mostly they arrive well after daybreak so the term 'dawn flight' is not really accurate. In Scotland in particular one of the roles of the professional goose guides is to locate a field or fields in which the geese are feeding. This can entail a considerable amount of driving as all the geese over a wide area are likely to congregate in a very limited number of places. Once the guide has found such a field he will probably return before dusk to make sure that they are still there. If they are, it is a near certainty that they will return the following morning and, with luck, bring a lot of their friends with them. It is a truly amazing sight to see so many geese, sometimes in thousands, congregating in a single field.

Even though the main flight will not come until well after dawn, it is customary for the shooter to be at the appointed field early so as to have plenty of time to put out the decoys and set up hides before the light comes. Not infrequently an early skein or two will attempt to come in whilst one is putting out the decoys. It is an extraordinary experience to be standing out in a broad field in the half light with pinkfeet whiffling down around one. Usually at this juncture someone makes a sprint to the field's edge for a gun. A futile exercise. By the time that it is to hand and loaded, the same pinkfeet are no more than tiny dots in the sky.

Whilst we divide our geese into the broad groupings of grey and black, in North America the division is into dark and white (light). The former group consists of the much sought-after Canada goose and the whitefront. It also includes the Brent, or Brant as it is known there. The snow goose and Ross's goose are the two main species of white geese. As is the case with ducks, daily bag limits tend to reflect the relative population strengths of the various species.

In recent years the Canada goose population in Britain has increased dramatically but the species has never been held in the same high esteem here as it is across the Atlantic. In North America it is a truly wild bird with all the mystery which surrounds a migrant species. In the UK and Ireland it is largely sedentary and often more than a touch on the tame side.

Snow goose – a species of 'white' goose (USA)

Blue phase snow goose

The population of Canada geese in the UK has expanded enormously in recent years, although their rating as a sporting quarry is not what it is in the USA.

CHAPTER ELEVEN

FLIGHTING AT DUSK

Time, it is said, passes slowly for those who have to wait. For this there is a simple reason: they have nothing to occupy themselves. But for the duck hunter settling into his place of concealment for evening flight, time will rarely drag. There are too many events of the closing day to keep him entertained until that first distant quack or whispering of wings announces the start of proceedings. These events fall naturally into two groups. There are those concerning the wild creatures which have been active during the day and are now about to quit the scene. And there are those concerning the creatures of the night. For these two sets of events the precise sequence, and indeed the players, will be dictated by location and time of year. And also, to some extent, by how the atmosphere is behaving.

We shall start on 1st September. Few serious duck hunters will be late for this first evening appointment of the new season. It has been many months, for some too many, since the prospect of black silhouettes crossing the darkening sky last set the adrenal glands in action. Being early autumn, the weather will probably be balmy and there should be a little heat left in the sun's rays as it sinks to the horizon. Insect life will still be plentiful and high above the water, swallows and martins will be engaging in their non-stop aerial acrobatics as they gather food for their final broods. These last chicks of the year must grow quickly if they are to successfully negotiate the long journey that awaits them. Every insect is vital and the parents will continue collecting them until evening is well advanced.

If there is a wood in the vicinity, a steady traffic of rooks and jackdaws will trundle across the sky to ancient roosts. From the four points of the compass they will come. Sometimes they fly directly into the trees. Other times they first gather in adjoining fields forming great black patches on the grass or stubbles. From these they will rise in noisy groups as dusk descends.

If there are reed beds surrounding the water there will be constant movement as reed buntings and warblers jockey for the best roosting spots. The warblers will not be with us for much longer: like the swallows and the martins they must soon leave for warmer wintering grounds.

Dusk approaches

Gradually, as the light fades, all this activity comes to an end. The birds of the day are now hopefully secure in their night-time quarters. But already, like shift workers in a factory, another group are taking over the watery places. In our local bog so many things are happening that it is well-nigh impossible to put them in chorological order. From the covers that enclose the far end, a couple of long-eared owls flap in leisurely manner over what is now their domain. Rats and voles, which betray their presence by a slight rustling in the long grass, are their primary concern. But, I suspect, an unwary snipe or teal may make an equally satisfactory meal. Overhead a final flight of black-headed gulls which nested in a neighbouring bog make their way to the river. They will soon be leaving the area. Having taken advantage of what the bog had to offer in order to raise their families they will seek out pastures new until spring is once more in the bog. At the water's edge the faintest 'plop' and concurrent ripple indicate that a water rail or moorhen is going about its nocturnal business. If there are trout in the water they will by now be feeding hungrily. The poor insects never stand a chance. No sooner have the swallows left the scene than the bats emerge. Big ones and small ones, they circle and dive erratically to capture these delectable morsels. I must confess that I have never learned to identify the various species. I know that there are Horseshoe bats, Long eared bats, Pipistrelles and a host of others. But which is which? Once a large bat swept high over my shoulder in the gathering gloom and had the misfortune to get shot in error for a teal. I have not made that error since but on more than one occasion the gun has been more than half way to the shoulder before realisation dawned that this was a bat and not a duck.

With so much to keep one entertained, there is the very real danger that concentration may flag and allow an early mallard or teal to slip in and land. This is where the snipe come in, where I live in Tipperary.

A flight pond in November: the swallows and martins have long gone but, unless it is very cold, bats may still be going about their business.

Almost invariably their appearance means that the ducks will not be too long delayed. In early September there may be only one or two of them but by November that characteristic screech and rush of displaced air is commonplace in the early dusk. They usually move only minutes before flight commences.

Let us now move on from that balmy September evening to a hard mid-winter dusk. It is likely we will be crouched behind whatever cover is available at the water's edge or, if the mercury has dropped below the zero mark, trying desperately to keep warm beside some spring-fed pond. The swallows and martins will have long since gone. But, surprisingly, unless it is very cold, bats may still be going about their business. Hungrier now and increasingly quarrelsome, the rooks are even noisier as they settle into their roosts. But the real harbinger of dusk now is the vixen. Her mind firmly focussed on thoughts of love, she is out and about at the first hint of nightfall. If the air is still, her screeching carries far. Just once in a while, if the wind is right and one keeps very still, she may make the ultimate mistake and wander into range.

Another mammal on the move at dusk is the otter. On one occasion, whilst standing with my back to a tall bush at the edge of a lake, my attention was drawn from scanning the distant sky by a strange hissing sound. Not ten yards away an otter was sitting up on its hind legs, rather after the manner of a begging dog, clearly objecting to my presence in this unusual way. On other occasions, particularly at the edge of floodwaters, I have experienced that strange sensation of being watched and, in quite close proximity, an otter has been viewing me with more than passing suspicion.

Small flights of cormorants are yet another reminder that dusk is not far off. More and more of them seem to be wintering inland. By day they pillage the trout stocks of the local rivers. By night they roost in surprising numbers in a few favoured trees along the river bank. It is not uncommon to see twenty or more silhouetted against the western sky. It is always easy to identify a tree in which cormorants roost. Invariably stained white with guano it will be dead or dying.

Before the last few tardy snipe make their appearance, two other birds are likely to be seen or heard. In winter vast flocks of curlews and lapwings are widespread and can be seen feeding and roosting in low-lying fields. As the light fails they come swishing across the water meadows. Both are likely to pitch in the shallows only to depart complaining noisily if the waiting hunter makes the slightest move.

Evening flight begins

Evening flight usually starts not too long after sunset. The first September flight comes near enough to 9pm where I live, a little later if the sky is clear and bright, a little earlier if it is dull and cloudy. Thereafter, the flight comes ever earlier with the shortening days. Two major factors can upset this time-honoured scheme of things: the moon and rain. In an earlier chapter I alluded to the fact that ducks tend to take to the wing later around the period of the full moon. Depending upon the time of moon rise, the flight may well be delayed by an hour or more at this time of the month. Rain, and especially heavy and consistent rain, is all but guaranteed to delay the flight. I do not think that I have ever seen a really good movement of ducks at dusk when rain is spilling from the Heavens.

Once underway, evening flight may be a brief affair, although there are times when it is prolonged. Early in the season it is most likely to be short. Unaccustomed to disturbance at their feeding grounds, ducks tend to come quickly at dusk. If encouragement has been provided in the form of a few fistfuls of barley in the shallows, the first birds are likely to put in an appearance while it is still quite bright. Later in the season matters are likely to be more protracted. Newly arrived teal and wigeon will move as soon as the light begins to fail whilst canny mallard, now well-versed in the ways of mankind, may wait for the protection of near-total darkness. There are times indeed when they come in so late that all that one is aware of is the splash caused by their landing.

Flighting at dusk is unquestionably the single biggest difference between the duck hunting traditions on the two sides of the Atlantic. This difference is then further magnified by the fact that in Europe we regard the feeding of flight ponds and such places as normal practice.

In a sense evening flight is every man's sport, because ducks seek out a great variety of places to feed and there are countless opportunities to lie in wait for them. Even well-fed and contented park mallard cannot resist

The evening flight usually starts not long after sunset. The first September flight comes at about 9pm where I live, a little later if the sky is clear and bright, a little earlier if it is dull and cloudy.

the genetic imprint which drives them out in search of pastures new in the failing light. We are talking of salt marshes and inland lakes, of bogs and flashes, of ponds and water meadows and a myriad of other watery places. For one man, evening flight may mean no more than a small pond in a field corner to which a handful of teal or mallard may come if the Gods decide to favour him. To another it may mean a well-stocked and well-fed flight pond, carefully tended and very sparingly shot where, at the end of the day, ducks of many species will surely pour in in waves.

A solitary pursuit

Whilst all sports have a social element, hunting as much as any other, there are times when, selfishly, I much prefer to be on my own or with a single companion. Evening flight is one such time. Most of my flighting haunts are relatively small and can be adequately covered by a single gun. Since ducks can come in from any angle, sometimes with little prior warning, it is much easier to be fully relaxed knowing that there is no danger to anyone else when one takes a shot. And, as every hunter knows, we only shoot really well when we are fully relaxed. I am personally very conscious of the fact that when I am shooting in close proximity to another gun I shoot less well.

There is, I think, a simple explanation for this. In all wing shooting there is one brief and optimum moment at which to pull the trigger. I find that if I am very near to someone, I tend to either shoot too soon or, worse still, wait until my neighbour has fired and then proceed to make a proper mess of what should be a comparatively straightforward shot.

Not much more than a mile from where I write there is a fine pond which covers the better part of an acre. Or, more accurately, there was a fine pond, because as a result of the construction of a new road, water levels recently dropped perilously low. At the moment we simply do not know whether it will ever return to its former glory. Less than two miles from this pond is a sanctuary lake and in September mallard from this lake religiously visit the pond at dusk. For the first few evenings of the new season up to half a dozen guns may lie in wait for them. It is a place where I rarely shoot well but for some unfathomable reason I make the occasional visit, though much less frequently than in the past. I will explain why. Around the pond the banks are mainly bare but there is a sufficiency of single bushes and clusters at irregular intervals to provide concealment.

The dogs are always keen to reach the bird first!

Effectively this means that the pond, whose diameter is nowhere greater than eighty or ninety yards, is surrounded by guns, not an ideal situation if one wants to be in a relaxed state of mind.

Early on, whilst there is still a reasonable amount of light in the sky, there is no real problem. Incoming birds are shot, or at least shot at, whilst they are still quite high. When they fall it is hard to resist a smile. From every point of the compass Labradors, retrievers, spaniels and other dogs of less certain pedigree launch themselves into the water to make the retrieve. I am always reminded of so many vapour trails converging on a single point. Because one shot a duck there is no guarantee whatsoever that one will, in the fullness of time, take possession of it. It is simply a question of 'let the best dog win'.

For a couple of seasons a man who owned a big black Labrador never failed to make an appearance at dusk. He was always amongst the first to arrive and invariably took up the best position. I never discovered just how good a shot he was but he always went away with a fine bag of mallard. None of our dogs could match the Labrador.

So far so good: still quite relaxed and shooting OK despite not retrieving most of the ducks that I have shot. My springer is fast but not fast enough. It is when the shadows lengthen that things begin to deteriorate rapidly at this particular pond. As is sometimes their wont, mallard can slip in low and unannounced. Almost invariably someone will fire, and this despite the fact that the bird is no more than a few feet above the water and the pond is surrounded. In theory everyone should know the location of everyone else so there should be no real danger. But the murmur of wings at dusk does wonders for one's adrenaline secretion and a rush of that hormone into the blood can cause strange deviations in human behaviour. Under such circumstances I must confess that I have never had much confidence in the proposition that the guns across from me have my best interests at heart. Readers used to a somewhat more disciplined and sophisticated brand of flighting may well ask the question, 'Why bother going to that particular pond if it is as bad as that?' Fair question. The only answer that I can give is that, just once in a while, no one else turns up and one can enjoy a first class flight.

To the uninitiated it might seem unlikely that a grassy field can have the capacity to yield a worthwhile flight of ducks, especially if there are some attractive-looking waters near at hand. But, unlikely as it may seem, it is sometimes the case that the said field does just that. One qualification is however necessary: it is most likely that the grassy field was recently flooded and the waters have just receded. There is nothing that grazing ducks (mainly wigeon) like better than a good sward of succulent grass, not too high and with just the slightest hint of water at the base of the shoots. The potential of such places was brought home to me quite forcibly many years ago. One November on the Ouse Washes the first floods of autumn had quickly receded so, for our duck shooting, we resorted to plan B. This consisted of waiting at the edge of the reed beds that fringed the Ouse in the hope that a few mallard would have the common decency to put in an appearance. There was always the off-chance of a teal or two as well. Wigeon though hardly ever came in. The deep waters of the river and the reed beds were not to their liking.

One particular evening mid-way through that November, the mallard and teal had singularly failed to oblige. It was a clear evening with rather more than a hint of frost and the western sky was shot with crimson as darkness began to fall. Having decided that there was little point in hanging on, we were standing and talking about whatever young men normally talk about when we spotted a pack of some dozen duck silhouettes. They were crossing the red horizon just above the flood wall on the opposite bank of the river and diving down into a field which, only a few days previously, had been a positive sea of water. At this juncture there was no point in further investigation. As every duck hunter quickly learns, there are few things more counter-productive than approaching a flighting spot once flight is underway. So plans were quickly laid. We would return in good time the following evening.

Next day conditions for flighting could not have been better when we arrived well ahead of schedule. It was overcast and breezy and there was no sign of the frost that had threatened the previous evening. Out in the middle of an exceptionally big field, a few flashes (puddles would probably be a more apt description) had clearly been the subject of some very special attention. Fresh wigeon feathers were scattered everywhere and in places the grass had been flattened down by what was surely a small army of ducks. Our only problem was a total lack of cover. Whilst during the high floods we could stand in under the boundary ditches for morning flight, out there there was not so much as a hefty tussock to hide behind. The only consolation was that, as is often the case at evening flight, a point comes in the gathering darkness when cover becomes a little less important. All we could do was crouch or kneel some fifty yards apart facing the dying brightness in the western sky. For my part it was, and always has been, a matter of kneeling. I can shoot reasonably well from this position but I have never mastered the art of standing up quickly from a crouching position and then swinging a shotgun sweetly.

We did not have to wait long. Snipe were still diving in all around us when the first whistling pack arrived. They seemed totally unfazed by the black 'lumps' so near to their intended points of descent. Once the flight started they came and they came. It seemed for a while as if every wigeon on the Washes had decided to pay a visit. We shot a lot of them that evening, probably – no, certainly – rather more than we would in this more conservation-orientated age.

Two evenings later, such is the naivety of youth, we returned to the same field in the full expectation of a repeat performance on the part of the wigeon. The puddles, though smaller, were still there but of fresh wigeon feathers there were precious few. Momentarily in the early dusk our spirits soared when a single wigeon appeared, started to circle and fell to the combined shot charges of two guns. But that was it. Not so much as one other wigeon called from the skies.

Falling flood

Since that day long ago I have always awaited the falling flood with more than passing impatience. Down the years one field in particular has been especially kind to me. It extends to some 25 acres and lies in a loop of the river Suir only a few miles from my home The centre of the field is a little lower than its extremities and in times past held water for much of the winter once the first flood came. Some years ago however the land changed hands and the new owner cut a deep drain from the field's lowest point to the river. As a result the floodwater levels now rise and fall with the river level. Despite this, once the soil becomes saturated by early winter the slightest hint of water remains beneath the grass for a few days after the river has fallen back. Not only do the wigeon come during these brief interludes but teal and mallard as well.

Frost

Frost, and by frost I mean serious frost, brings a new dimension to evening flight. If the cold snap is not too prolonged, a week or so at most, it can do wonders for shooting. The number of places that ducks can visit at dusk becomes dramatically reduced so that selecting a likely spot for flight becomes rather less than a lottery. As well as this there is the very real likelihood that more ducks than usual will come in. But should the hard weather persist for too long they are likely to desert many of their normal haunts and make for the comparative mildness of the coast. Worse still, and this is especially true of teal, the condition of those that remain inland can deteriorate quickly. Sensibly, most countries have legislation in place that provides for the introduction of a temporary shooting ban under such conditions.

Weather and duck shooting

Despite the close proximity of Britain and Ireland, British winters tend to be more severe than Irish ones. This is especially true if one compares the east of England with the west of Ireland. January isotherms say it all most eloquently. In the case of Britain, anticyclonic conditions over mainland Europe have a habit of extending an icy grip in its direction. The nature of Irish winters, in contrast, is largely dictated by the country's proximity to the comparatively mild waters of the Atlantic. These differences may become less pronounced in the years ahead if the signs of global warming now all around us are anything to go by.

Presently, as we have seen, ducks move from mainland Europe to Britain in response to bouts of hard weather. And should that harsh weather spread to Britain, they move westwards again to Ireland. If European winters get milder all this may change and, from the duck hunter's perspective, change very much for the worse.

When the mercury really plummets, the sorts of places to head for towards evening are spring-fed ponds and bogs, small rivers that widen into ponds at intervals, marshy fields crisscrossed by streams, slow flowing rivers and the like. Anywhere in fact where the water's movement is sufficient to prevent it from freezing over. An extraordinary variety of wetland birds can congregate in such places at the hour of dusk.

In addition to the ducks there will be the almost inevitable snipe, curlews and lapwings. If there is a sufficiency of free water, whooper swans and grey herons are likely to visit. Golden plovers may come as well. At one of my favourite spots, woodcock come hurtling down across the water heading for an adjacent marshy field. Then there are the starlings. If there are reed beds or clusters of bushes in the vicinity they may come to roost in their thousands.

Waiting for ducks to flight on these evenings can be a chilly affair. The warmth gained from the car's heater or generated by a brisk walk across the fields is quickly lost once one's motion ceases. The best-wrapped toes soon begin to tingle, especially if their owner has elected to stand in water. Fingers, too, quickly move on from being cold to being painfully cold. Some people are just plain lucky. They can shoot equally well with or without gloves. I cannot. Shooting gloves and I have never agreed. I have tried the ones which cover everything except the top two joints of the trigger finger. I especially hate these. They cause all the pain to focus at the top of that particular finger.

Flight can start early on those frosty evenings. Teal, as usual, will be the first to arrive. With minds concentrated by hunger, they are quite likely to dispense with the customary circuit and dive straight in. This can be more than a little

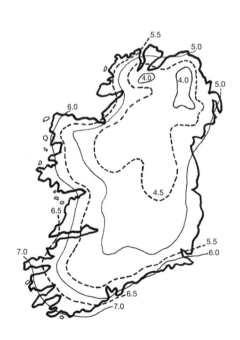

January isotherms for Ireland (°C)

disconcerting as, unless there is a clear background, they may well touch down before one has a chance to raise the gun. 101% concentration is the only answer. Mallard, too, are liable to come straight in.

One aspect of mallard behaviour has always puzzled me when temperatures are on the low side. On occasions they seem totally oblivious to the fact that the chosen water is covered by a sheet of ice. Touching down with wings spread wide in normal landing mode they end up on their backsides and shoot off across the slippery surface. I can understand this happening

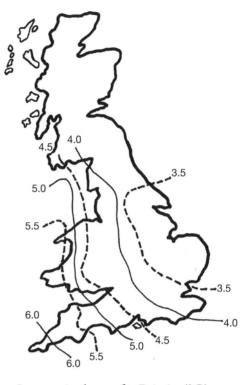

January isotherms for Britain (°C)

on the first evening of a big freeze but I have witnessed repeat performances on successive nights. Maybe it is just that mallard are not quite as bright as I would like to think they are.

Before leaving the subject of evening flight there are two matters that must be addressed. One of these relates to the coastal gunner, the other to the matter of retrieving.

The coastal gunner

For the man who plies his trade beyond the sea wall there are a number of potential hazards that need serious consideration. Unlike his inland counterpart he may well have to negotiate a number of muddy creeks as he makes his way to his chosen spot for evening flight. In some parts he may have to travel a considerable distance if he is to have a reasonable chance of intercepting a flight line. It is vital that he knows the area, the times of the tides and the speed with which the incoming tide fills the creeks that he has crossed. It is bad enough having to negotiate swiftly-filling creeks by the light of day: in darkness it can be quite a frightening prospect. Been there, done that, and have no wish for a repeat performance.

I once shot with a man who I had always regarded as the most solid and sensible of citizens. I have since revised that assessment. One evening he took me to his favourite flighting spot which, in retrospect, seemed to be a very long way from the sea wall. On the way out we crossed a number of nearly empty but threateningly deep creeks. Seeing concern written all over my face he assured me that he had consulted the tide tables and that we would be back on *terra firma* long before there would be any cause for alarm. In fairness to the man, we shot a fair bag of wigeon that evening. But there the fairness stops. While there was still a hint of brightness in the sky he plodded across to the creek in which I was concealed and said that we would have to 'run for it now' as the tide had turned. Running on soft mud is not easy. Running on soft mud wearing waders and carrying a shotgun and a bundle of ducks is anything but easy. Before we were half way back, the creeks were swirling with water topped with white foam, my heart was beating somewhere near to 200 to the minute and I was giving serious consideration to dumping the gun and ducks. Eventually, by the grace of God, we reached solid ground. Quite nonchalantly my companion turned to me and said, 'I told you that we would have no problem with the tide.' It would be lacking in delicacy to consign my reply to print.

Fog is another hazard for the coastal fowler. At times it can sweep in off the sea with unnerving speed. Nothing is more guaranteed to put the fear of God into one than being way out on the mud, dusk descending, visibility down to a few yards and literally not knowing the way to safety. Again, been there, done that. Moral of the story: never ever go out on the mud without a compass.

Thinking back to my erstwhile friend mentioned above, I am of the view that we all meet a few lunatics in the course of our lives. In my own case I think that I have met rather more than my fair share. One comes to mind who invited me to go fishing with him. I still shudder when I look back on that particular episode. At that time our family was young and we had a big and clumsy caravan which I used to tow down to the sea each summer. One evening we pulled into the usual caravan park and set up shop next to a caravan that I had not seen there before. I soon got talking to the owner, a kindred spirit with a passion for both rod and gun. He told me that he knew a 'fabulous' place to catch mackerel and pollock and that it was at its best when the full tide coincided with dusk.

A few evenings later he took me to the fabulous spot. We had driven for about five miles when he pulled into a tiny car park – it accommodated at most three cars – on the top of a cliff. Having unloaded his gear he hopped over a barrier in front of the car and said, 'Down here'. Down here was a precipitous slope of a few hundred feet with a gradient of something like one in one and a half. My new-found friend then proceeded to go down with all the alacrity of a spider descending its web to eat a trapped fly. He controlled his descent one handed by hanging on to the odd piece of protruding rock or tussock of vegetation. I had little option but to follow suit. At the base of the cliff was a large flat rock which provided an excellent stand for fishing. We caught the proverbial bag of pollock but I did not enjoy the experience one bit. It was getting dark and my thoughts were focussed solely on climbing up that perilous rock face. Somehow I made it, but never again. When, about a week later, I received another invitation to accompany this particular lunatic on a fishing expedition, I discovered that my appointment book was full.

Retrieving

Finally to retrieving or more precisely, when to do the retrieving. Evening flight can be a fairly concentrated affair, often with little time between the arrival of different ducks or different packs of ducks. Because of this there can be the very real temptation to hold back the dog for fear of frightening off incoming birds. My view on this is quite simple. One can never be sure that a shot bird is dead. However hard it may appear to hit land or water, it is not an uncommon experience to find it very much alive and doing its best to escape or hide. As sportsmen there is an onus on us to retrieve it and despatch it as quickly as possible. Consequently, even if it means foregoing a shot or two, the dog should be sent out straightaway once a bird is down.

The only exception that I would make is the case of the pricked bird that glides down a good distance away. In an ideal world one would always have a non-shooting companion who could set out and retrieve it. In the less than perfect world which we inhabit, the bird should be carefully marked and every attempt should be made to find it as soon as the flight is over.

CHAPTER TWELVE

MOONLIGHT

Shooting under the moon is really an extension, sometimes much delayed, of evening flight. The difference is that once the light has deteriorated to a certain point, the night gets no darker. As a result the action can go on much longer, on occasions very much longer.

Between the moons, the timing of evening flight is reasonably predictable. Much less so though once first quarter has passed. A lot depends upon the time of moonrise. If it is already high in the sky before dusk there may be little difference from the normal starting time. But if the moon does not break the horizon for a period after nightfall, the flight is likely to be well delayed. In this latter situation very little may happen at dusk. The odd mallard or teal, anxious to get on with the serious business of feeding, may move, but the great majority of ducks, and wigeon in particular, will tend to bide their time. They may wait until the moon is quite high before taking to the wing. The wild geese feed on under the moon instead of returning to their roosts at dusk.

The number of opportunities for moon flighting in any one month is usually limited. This is because the sky must be just right. A cloudless sky is useless. Away from the immediate brightness of the moon there is nothing but inky blackness interrupted only by twinkling stars. You can hear the murmur of wings, the birds are often in range but for 99%

of the time they are invisible. Few things in my experience are more frustrating than to hear ducks overhead and yet be unable to see them. Twice, and only twice, I have given way to that frustration and fired. On both occasions by the most extraordinary of chances I met with success.

The first of these occasions was long ago in the bog where the villain shot my decoys. It was an evening early in January and some ducks were already in residence when I reached the floodwater. The moon had risen some two hours previously. All around me wigeon were whistling and the sky was full of the rushing sound of displaced air. Far out across the bog the call of curlews reached an occasional crescendo. Overhead and unseen, single birds and packs were going about their nocturnal business secure against the blackness of the sky. I had been there for about twenty minutes when the whistle of a cock wigeon caused me to look directly towards the moon.

The number of opportunities for moon flighting in any one month is usually limited. This is because the sky must be just right. A cloudless sky is useless.

For the briefest of moments I saw the best part of a dozen silhouettes crossing in front of it. As they were disappearing into the glooming I threw my gun to my shoulder and fired a single shot at where I thought the last bird should be. Two things then happened simultaneously. There was a positive roar of wings as fowl of every type exited the bog at knots and a number of splashes indicated that my shot had found its mark.

Within a minute, and much to my surprise, the dog returned with a curlew. He then went out again and returned with a second one. In somewhat less than good humour I sent him out once more. After a short delay he brought me back a fine cock wigeon, surely the most unlucky wigeon in Christendom. I could only assume that this unfortunate wigeon had thrown in its lot with a flock of curlews. I have seen mixed packs of wigeon and pintail. Much less frequently I have seen wigeon consorting with mallard or teal. But never before or since have I seen wigeon flying in the company of curlews.

Some years later in very different surroundings I again shot a duck under the moon when there was not so much as a single cloud in the sky. Just behind my house the ground rises steadily for about 150 feet to a small plateau. The whole area is set with corn every year. In those days the plateau housed a smallish flash pond in a hollow which usually persisted until the coming of the drying winds of spring. The pond could usually be relied upon to deliver a few mallard or teal as long as it was not shot too often. Wigeon only rarely visited it and then not before the turn of the year. When they did come they were attracted by the succulent young barley or wheat plants. On the night in question it was again cloudless and the moon was only a couple of nights short of full. About 8.30pm the dogs began barking and were showing no intention of stopping. When I went out to quieten them I became instantly aware of what was clearly a big assembly of teal.

A quite extraordinary volume of piping was coming from the pond on top of the hill. Those primeval instincts that determine the ways of the hunter promptly took over. Within minutes I was off with gun and dog to the pond. It was conveniently situated no more than twenty yards out from the ditch. I say 'was' because that particular pond is no more. Despite the fact that at its biggest it never occupied a rood of ground, it was drained a couple of years back in the interests of 'progress'. As I approached along the far side of the ditch the sheer amount of sound emanating from the pond confirmed that there were a lot of teal in residence. A small gap in the ditch allowed access to the field in which the pond was located. I had barely made my way through this gap when what could only be described as an eruption took place. A lot of black objects too numerous to count tore into the sky. Not unlike my situation with the wigeon many years previously, or more accurately what I believed to be wigeon, I was momentarily aware of these objects before they vanished into the blackness. I fired a single shot and was rewarded with the sight of one of their number tumbling to earth. It was a big cock teal in full plumage.

I learned an important lesson that night. Flushing and shooting ducks from a small pond by moonlight is not a good idea. Unsurprisingly it does little for their confidence in the place. Many weeks elapsed before I again saw teal on that pond.

Ideal cloud conditions

For moon flighting, the cloud cover must be just right. Heavy, dark clouds are almost as bad as a cloudless sky. What one wants is a complete cover of light, fleecy clouds against which the ducks will be clearly silhouetted. An accompanying good stiff breeze is no bad thing either. As well as keeping the birds low it helps to dissipate the sound of shooting. Somehow, though it may be just my imagination, the crackle of shotgun fire seems magnified on a still moonlit night.

If the moon is anywhere near full and the cloud sufficiently light it is possible to see ducks at a great distance, certainly a few hundred yards. But estimating range on these nights is far from easy, especially on an open marsh or suchlike where there are no trees or shrubs to use as markers. And, it must not be forgotten, if it is easy for the hunter to see his quarry it is at least as easy for the potential quarry to spot any threats to its wellbeing. At dawn and dusk an exposed face is always a big giveaway. More so under the moon.

When flighting ducks under the moon there is really one of two options. Either, if one is lucky enough to find one, to await their coming at a feeding place or, alternatively, to take up a likely position in anticipa-

For moon flighting the cloud cover must be just right. Heavy, dark clouds are almost as bad as a cloudless sky. What one wants is a complete cover of light, fleecy clouds against which the ducks will be clearly silhouetted.

tion of getting a few shots at passing birds. This latter proposition is not as haphazard as it may sound. Where there are extensive salt marshes or, inland, substantial areas of floodwater there can be ducks on the move for most of the night. It is my belief that they tend to become somewhat disorientated in the brightness and begin to wander rather than spending the night at a single location.

Make no mistake about it, this night shooting demands stamina. Winter nights can be cold affairs as one quickly discovers on an open marsh. It also requires a high degree of concentration. In a typical scenario one goes to the appointed spot in time for dusk even though there will likely be little movement of fowl at this hour. However, there is always the chance of a shot or two. Assuming that the moon has not yet risen there is then nothing for it but to wait for the horizon to begin to brighten. What happens next is very much in the lap of the Gods. Some nights the moon will be barely up before ducks take to the wing. On other nights there may be a long wait in store for one. Usually, once a flight develops, one can expect a lively opening session. After that, and depending upon how attractive the area is for fowl, packs are likely to be on the move at irregular intervals. Some people head for home once the main traffic appears to have ceased. This can be a mistake as patience is now truly a virtue. A wait will nearly always be rewarded.

On the coast a strong running tide can sometimes work wonders, especially if high water comes a little after the moon is up. Already restless with the brightness, wigeon are often that extra bit anxious to get airborne with this additional prompting.

Can you shoot all night under the moon? The answer to this is very much in the affirmative. When in our student days we shot over the Ouse Washes we used to stay out for literally hours. Sheer fatigue rather than a lack of ducks was the usual reason for calling a halt to proceedings. On many a night we lingered on until midnight and beyond in the hope of yet another whistling pack. There was one memorable night when we shot until 3am and there was still some movement when we were leaving. In my experience of moonflighting the bag is composed predominantly of wigeon. When the flight first gets underway there will be a variety of ducks on the move but as the hours pass it is mainly wigeon that are flying. On the Washes there would be pintail as well, sometimes in discrete packs, other times mixed in with the wigeon. I must confess that on the occasions on which I shot a pintail under the moon I thought it to be a wigeon until I had it in my hand.

CHAPTER THIRTEEN

STUBBLE TIME

The most successful wild creatures are those that have a capacity to adapt to new surroundings, often drastically different from their traditional ones, and to exploit new food sources. In this respect wildfowl, surely amongst the wildest of all God's creatures, have few equals. In comparatively recent times a number of species have responded positively to environmental changes wrought by the hand of man. The enthusiasm with which tufted ducks and Canada geese took to flooded gravel pits is a case in point.

But it is in the realm of agriculture that ducks and geese have been especially quick to adapt. Once potato growing became a large-scale and widespread enterprise in Scotland, greylags and pinkfeet were not found wanting. Sugar beet too was a crop they found very much to their liking. In the 1920s, Greenland white-fronts, which fed upon the rough vegetation of the great bogs of central and western Ireland, discovered the more succulent grasses being grown on the Wexford Slobs. Gradually they began to desert their bogland homes in favour of these two polders. More recently, also in county Wexford, the pale bellied Brent geese started to feed on winter cereals in place of their centuries-old diet of eel grass.

It is however corn, and barley in particular in this part of the world, that has come to elicit the greatest interest. In their eagerness to partake of this annual feast, mallard do not confine their feeding visits to the safety of the twilight hours and darkness. If not disturbed they will visit barley fields on and off throughout the day. Indeed they do not necessarily even wait for the harvest to be completed. When in wild and wet summers which result in the barley crop being flattened (lodged), they have an uncanny knack of locating the stricken crop within hours. Fortunately for the farmer, but unfortunately for ducks, lodging is less of a problem nowadays. This is due to the development of shorter and stronger stemmed cereal plants.

Even if there is no lodging, mallard will sometimes come to a field of standing corn to feed. This is something of which I only became aware a couple of years ago. At the time we were growing potatoes on the farm. In one particular field there had been a few acres of early varieties next

Mallard feeding on September barley stubble.

178

to a crop of spring barley. By mid-August the early potatoes had been cleared leaving bare clay next to the barley which was not quite ready for the combine. One morning I noticed a fair flight of mallard descending on the field. They did not circle before pitching in which suggested that they had been visiting for a while. I assumed that their interest lay in the small and damaged tubers scattered on the ground. But this was not the case. Watching from a distance it was quite clear that the potatoes were not the attraction. Having landed some twenty or thirty yards out from the edge of the barley, they began to waddle towards it. Some of them in fact were almost running. Then, literally on tip toe with necks stretched to a maximum, they proceeded to pull down and devour the heads of grain. This performance was repeated every day until the corn was cut. On the day that the combines moved into the field they made several abortive attempts to come in whilst they were operating. Then, when the combines finally left the field, they were back once more.

Most of the dabbling ducks will feed on spilled grain but I have rarely shot species other than mallard over stubbles. Teal will readily come to a flight pond that is being fed with barley but I can think of no more than a handful of occasions when I have shot them in a stubble field. Pintail will certainly come to stubbles but I have little experience of shooting them in this situation. They do not visit Ireland in very large numbers and those that do come remain largely on the coast. Once, on the Wexford Slobs, I was shooting from a hide at the edge of a wide channel. Across from me on the other bank were several hundred acres of stubbles. With more than passing jealously I sat and watched one early October morning as a gentleman there took down more than a dozen pintail in the course of the morning. This was the only time that I witnessed a substantial flight of these elegant ducks into stubbles. Needless to say not one of them saw fit to come to my side of the channel!

Hereabouts, of recent years, two factors have militated against stubble flighting. The first is the very large area now being devoted to winter corn. Well before September has run its course, the plough has done its worst and the stubbles are no more. By mid-November the tiny green shoots of next year's crop are well in evidence. The second is the enormous expansion in the populations of opportunistic species, in particular rooks, jackdaws and wood pigeons. So numerous have the crows become that they are an increasing threat to newly-drilled corn. There are fields in this area that literally turn black with crows as soon as the new shoots emerge. In this respect, how very different things seem to be in eastern Scotland. Rooks and jackdaws seem to be much less plentiful and there is sufficient spilled grain lying in the stubbles to hold the interest of the grey geese through October and even into the early days of November.

Mallard can be very conservative in their selection of stubble fields. They are likely to visit the same ones year after year and studiously ignore nearby ones which, at least to the human eye, appear identical. In this respect they mirror the behaviour of golden plover later in the autumn. They too confine their attentions almost exclusively to certain fields. As a general rule mallard prefer broad fields to smaller ones and prefer to feed well away from ditches. If the area is not subject to too much disturbance they are likely to rely on stubbles fairly close to their roosting waters. But once subjected to shooting they will soon give those fields a wide berth and seek out quieter fields, often a considerable distance away.

Other than showing a preference for the parts of a field well removed from any cover, there seems to be little selectivity as to the precise part that they will visit On several occasions on the eve of a new season I have watched mallard coming in at dusk with the intention of setting up camp in the chosen vicinity the following dawn. More often than not they have selected another part of the field next morning.

Unless one is fortunate enough to live in an area where disturbance is minimal, stubble flighting quickly becomes a dawn and dusk affair once the season opens. The dawn flight to stubble ground can come very early. If the mallard were deprived of their fix of barley the previous evening they are likely to be on the move well before first light. In order to get there ahead of them it is necessary to set off whilst it is still very dark. One early September morning I had, or so I thought, arrived on the stubbles with plenty of time to spare. But, walking across the field in total darkness, I became quickly aware of ducks taking off all around me, quacking in indignation. As usual that morning I lay out where the stubbles were high on a patch of undulating ground. It was still too dark to see. Within minutes more ducks arrived and pitched in quite near to me. It was a quite extraordinary experience to be lying there in the dark with the chattering of feeding ducks just yards away. Eventually the sky brightened a little and I sat up fully expecting to get a couple of shots. It was not to be, however. Sound can travel a long way on the still morning air and the assembled throng took off with a roar of wings well out of range. Not surprisingly they did not come back to those stubbles again that autumn.

If mallard visit stubbles in the evening, it is more or less certain that they will return again at dawn provided that they were not disturbed. What is rather less certain is the manner of their return. Ideally they will flight in twos and threes and small packs. In my experience however, this does not happen too often. Far more likely there will be the almost inevitable single bird and then a small number of sizeable packs. The worst case scenario is when they all come together in one great rush of wings and proceed to settle well away from you. Early in the season they may not be deterred by the first volley of shots. Such is their fondness for barley that

The worst case scenario: a large pack of mallard arrive all at once on a field of barley stubble and settle too far away from the waiting gun.

they may well attempt a second visit within fifteen or twenty minutes. The problem now is that it is likely to be quite bright so the only hope is to seek the cover of a ditch. Having been disturbed earlier, they are likely to circle before pitching and may thus provide a few shots. If there has been a good flight at dawn there is always the temptation to make a second foray to the field at dusk. This should be avoided. A second baptism of fire on the one day is a guaranteed method of persuading them to feed elsewhere. Realistically one has to make a choice with stubble flighting: morning or evening. And, not only that, the ducks must be given a few days to recover their confidence before attempting a repeat performance.

Stubble shooting in North America is a little different. This, I suspect, is due to the origin of the ducks. In Britain and Ireland we are shooting locally bred birds and numbers are rarely what could be described as enormous. Early in the season I would rate it a great flight if anything in excess of a hundred ducks attempted to come in at dawn. Thereafter a couple of dozen are likely to be about par for the course. In contrast, on the vast American stubble grounds, local populations can be augmented by countless migrants as they move steadily south. With this great annual movement the sheer number of ducks is frequently far greater than anything we are likely to see here. As well as this, whereas our flight is over and done with before full daylight, our transatlantic counterparts can be confronted by waves of mallard, often newly arrived, well into the day.

On balance my preference is to flight stubbles at dusk. There are a number of reasons for this. For a start concealment in very open places becomes less of a problem with the fading light. One can initially use the cover of a ditch and then move out into the field as dusk descends. In the same way that ducks are likely to be on the move early in the morning, they can grow impatient in the evening and start flighting to stubble ground whilst it is still quite bright. But the greatest bonus provided by waiting until evening is the fact that they are likely to come in smaller groups and thus provide more shooting. I cannot provide any ready explanation for this but I have nearly always found it to be the case.

I have rarely found the moon to be beneficial when it comes to stubble flighting. When it is near to full at the hour of dusk, the ducks, in my experience, tend to come a little earlier than at other times of the month. On those nights on which moonrise comes some hours after dusk they will flight to stubbles. But one has to be very lucky to get the sort of shooting which is possible under the moon over salt marshes and flood-waters later in the year.

Heads up and obviously ill at ease – this group of mallard is unlikely to remain in the stubbles for long.

CHAPTER FOURTEEN

PUNT GUNNING

Once the shotgun had been developed there was a certain inevitability that bigger and bigger ones would be produced. There is little doubt that demand for these great weapons first came from commercial hunters. For them the possibility of coming to terms with the vast rafts of wigeon and other ducks bobbing contentedly up and down on sheltered bays and the massed ranks of geese on the sand bars must have been a mouth-watering prospect.

But the punt gun as we know it probably had a long gestation. In his book *The History of Wildfowling*, John Marchington makes the point that there were no true punt guns until around 1800. Before that date an assembly of mini cannons were either shore-based or fired from a boat as opposed to a punt.

Despite the romance surrounding punt gunning which is deeply embedded in the wildfowling tradition, it was and is a dangerous occupation. The punt has a very shallow draught and this, coupled with the weight of the gun, which is up to 170 pounds, means that any excursion other than on the flattest of waters is hazardous in the extreme.

A typical punt is just under twenty feet in length. For propulsion a pole or paddles are used, the latter when in sight of fowl and manoeuvring for a shot. The gunner lies on his stomach and operates the paddles underwater in order to minimise the risk of disturbing the birds. If possible he would like to get within sixty yards before firing. But, more often than not, he is content to take the shot at between sixty and ninety yards. Double (two man) punts were sometimes used. Freed from the chore of propelling the punt, the gunner was able to devote his full attention to firing at the most appropriate moment. This, in theory, is when the birds are in the initial stage of take off and when, with wings open, they are at their most vulnerable.

It is most probable that the first punt guns were fired from the shoulder. But then, inevitably, they reached a size at which even the most burly of human frames could not absorb the recoil. We are talking of guns with barrels in excess of eight feet and a bore of at least one inch. These mighty weapons were capable of throwing a lethal shot charge weighing as much as one and a half pounds over a hundred yards. To take the recoil, the gun, which lies along the foredeck of the punt, is secured to it by ropes. For this purpose the gun has two lateral projections called trunnions on which to attach the ropes.

Basically the gun is aimed by aligning the punt in the right direction, no easy task bearing in mind the influence of tide and waves. Greater sophistication was achieved in some cases by use of a loose swivel or by use of a swivel permanently attached to the barrels.

Part of the essential equipment of the punt gunner is the cripple stopper. This is an ordinary twelve bore shotgun used to pick off the inevitable wounded birds. In the annals of punt gunning there are many horrific accounts of mishaps with the cripple stopper. These include accidental discharges which wounded either the gunner or his puntsman or caused the punt to sink when a hole was blown in the floor.

Contrary to popular belief, big bags were not that common. For a successful outing the weather had to be just right. Wind and rain militated against the puntsman and even on still mornings fog could be a major

The puntgunner's craft: low on the water and battleship grey in colour. The long-barrelled gun rests across the bow, pointing in the direction of the quarry.

problem. It was not uncommon for him to be confined to land for days on end, something that clearly did little for his cash flow. Even on those days when it was possible to put to sea, there was no guarantee of success. Wigeon in particular are never that keen to allow a close approach.

Before the advent of the breech-loader in the middle of the 19th century, the returning gunner who had not been successful in getting a shot had something of a dilemma. Unloading the gun was not really a practical proposition. The dilemma was usually resolved by discharging the gun into the packed masses of wading birds such as curlews and godwits that feed on the tideline. Godwit, I think I once read, is a corruption of good to eat. These larger wading birds commanded a reasonable price on the markets but nowhere near that which was obtained for ducks and geese.

During the 19th century, and particularly towards its end, punt gunning became the chosen sport of a small and wealthy elite. In this respect the exploits of one, Sir Ralph Payne-Gallwey, figure large in wildfowl lore. Brent geese and wigeon were very much his favoured quarry. Today punt gunning is the sport of very few. The commercial gunners of old have long since departed the scene. Marchington records that at the end of the Second World War there were only 105-150 punts operating in England and 20-30 in Scotland. Since then numbers have dwindled considerably. In Britain punt gunning remains a legitimate activity with the proviso that, since the enactment of the 1954 Wild Bird Protection Act, the maximum bore does not exceed 1.75 inches. In Ireland, following the passage into law of the 1976 Wildlife Act, only those who held a licence before that year are still entitled to one. Literally only a tiny number of these are left.

As the puntgunner closes in on his quarry he will use paddles, or just his hands, to propel the punt forwards, keeping a low profile at all times.

CHAPTER FIFTEEN

THE FUTURE

If, as I believe it will, the sport of duck shooting is to prosper in the years ahead, two major issues will require continuous address. The first of these is the political one. It is not my intention in this book to dwell on it. Suffice to say that individuals and their representative associations must be ever on guard because there are sections of the 'anti' movement who will do anything, within the law or without the law, to try to bring an end to our sport. Should anyone be complacent, or have the slightest doubt about the activities of these people, I can do no better than point to the Australian States of New South Wales and Queensland. In each of these, powerful anti-hunting lobbies have been successful in bringing about a ban. And major battles lie ahead in other parts of Australia as well.

The second issue may at first glance appear so simplistic as to be hardly worthy of comment. Simplistic it certainly is but how we address it is vital, not least because it cannot be fully divorced from matters political. I refer to having sufficient ducks to shoot. Mention has already been made of the threats posed to wild populations by commercial hunting and habitat loss. To these must now be added an increasing demand for leisure activities. More people than ever before are taking up shooting. It is also likely that minor climatic changes have had a detrimental effect on some species. In Europe this is best exemplified by the fate of the grey partridge. It has declined right across its range and appears to still be so doing. Remedial measures centred initially upon importation of fresh stocks from countries where the species was still faring reasonably well. Coupled with this an increasing emphasis was placed upon the release of birds reared in captivity. This practice has now become the norm and it is no exaggeration to say that most partridges and pheasants that fall to sportsmen's guns started life in an incubator. Indeed without these annual 'top ups' a lot of people would have precious little shooting.

Reared mallard

With wild ducks the situation is different but not completely different. Migratory populations are holding their own and providing a shootable surplus. However one species, the mallard, bears the brunt of shooting pressures. More mallard are shot in Britain and Ireland every year than all other wild duck species combined. To sustain this level of shooting, a policy of rear and release is necessary. Fortunately the mallard has proved to be exceptionally amenable to captive breeding and the ducklings are easily reared. Strangely it seems to be the only duck species that lends itself to large-scale commercial production.

The danger as I see it is that the mallard could become just another 'pheasant' with all that that implies – 100-bird days, 200-bird days to order. And this brings us back to politics. Many people who have no problem with the rough shooter or wildfowler going about his business baulk at the more formal type of shooting where big numbers of released birds are shot on a regular basis. It is vital in my estimation for the future of our sport that we do not alienate this middle ground. The 'anti' faction is more than adept at misrepresentation and manipulation. We must, I believe, ensure that in everything we do we do not give them ammunition with which to win the hearts and minds of the middle ground.

By all means let us continue with mallard releases, but not in vast numbers. Ideally the primary purpose of such releases should be to increase the wild breeding stock. There is little doubt in my mind that the future of duck hunting will be best assured by improving existing habitats and, where possible, by creating new ones. To this end it is necessary to have a clear understanding of what we mean by habitat. It is essentially an amalgam of physical and biological components which meet all the life requirements of a given species. Water, oxygen and temperature are examples of physical components. Biological components include other organisms which are essential as food sources. In the case of birds, plants are vital for the provision of nest sites or simply as cover in which to hide from predators. When planning a campaign of habitat work, all these components must be taken into account.

Pollution and global warming

In the modern era few habitats have become more threatened than wetland ones. Drainage has long since taken a toll. Fortunately this may no longer be the serious issue it once was. Greatly increased agricultural efficiency

A newly-created duck lake: planting is of vital importance in making the right habitat for ducks, with plenty of good nesting sites and protection from predators.

and a much heightened sense of environmental awareness means that there is now a greater willingness to leave wet places alone. Pollution of these places, however, remains a problem. Untreated or imperfectly treated sewage is widely discharged into rivers, lakes and the sea. Agricultural effluents still find their way into natural water bodies where, like sewage, they precipitate a chain of events which results in long term and not easily reversible damage. The discharge of waste oil by shipping poses yet another threat to wildfowl and their habitats. I could go on.

Yet another threat to natural habitats has now emerged in the form of global warming. Until quite recently the great majority of us did not take the issue seriously. It was something that long-haired boffins talked about knowledgeably on television and to which newspapers devote columns in those rare boring interludes when politicians are behaving themselves. But now we know that our planet is warming up and that we ourselves are responsible. We know what is happening, we know the implications and still we pour forth a frightening stream of greenhouse gases from our cars, planes, factories and power stations. For wildfowl the potential consequences could not be more serious. Vital habitats like salt marshes may be lost as the melting of polar ice results in rising sea levels. Breeding grounds are also under threat. Hotter summers are part and parcel of global warming so the likelihood of the breeding grounds drying out is very real.

On a different note, global warming may provoke profound changes in the migratory patterns of wildfowl. Will they, in the years ahead, linger much later on the breeding grounds? Will they need to journey as far south as is presently the case?

Practical steps for the wildfowler

Faced with problems of this magnitude, the individual duck shooter may well wonder if it is within his capacity to address the issues of habitat improvement in any meaningful way. The answer to this particular conundrum is that, despite the apparent magnitude of the task, there is much that he can do. The range of wetland habitats is enormous so I can do no more than present a few examples.

In one place the silting up of a shallow water body may have made it unattractive to wildfowl. This can be addressed by putting in the hard hours with the shovel or, better, with tractor and bucket. In another area, and this is especially true of still and slow-moving waters, the expansion of reed beds can be reversed. Reeds are invasive plants and their management is essentially an ongoing matter. They can be sprayed, cut, burned or rooted out. Personally I would opt for any method other than spraying. The less chemicals that we disperse into the environment the better as far as I am concerned. Some of the new generation of agricultural sprays are supposed to degrade in a short period of time. Maybe, but I have my doubts. Where physical 'adjustments' to a habitat are not a practical proposition or are not required, there other aspects that can be considered. The erection of nesting baskets on stilts or the construction of nesting rafts can help to increase natural productivity. Aquatic plants are important as food sources. They are surprisingly amenable to being transplanted. Some of them are also important as hosts to the insects which are vital components of the diet of ducklings.

Predator control

However, there is no doubt in my mind that the most important habitat work an individual can do lies in the control of species which damage duck stocks. Some people refer to these creatures as vermin. Others, with a hint of political correctness, call them predators. It is necessary to be very precise. Many animals take eggs and eat ducklings and adult birds. I am not suggesting that all should be culled. The day has long since gone, for example, when it was considered acceptable to kill each and every bird of prey that appeared in the sky. Note also that I use the word control. Our objective is to keep each of the offending populations within reasonable bounds: it is not a question of eradication. Because of this it is work which is never-ending. Many of these species are opportunistic by nature and have adapted all too well to an environment shaped by the hand of man.

The next-raiding magpie is a prime example. A clutch of seven or eight is about normal for this most lethal of predators. And the problem is that all the magpie eggs are likely to give rise to new adults. In sharp contrast it would be a very rare mallard or teal that laid eight eggs and

Predated mallard egg – a magpie was the probable culprit.

The Larsen trap: the most efficient method of magpie control.

then proceeded to rear eight ducklings. An added problem is that these opportunists are quick to locate new territories. If, as is frequently the case, one's neighbours are not approaching the matter with equal zeal, one is essentially providing a vacuum which the said neighbour's surplus will be only too happy to fill.

Predator control has to be undertaken all year round if it is to achieve the desired effect. Compensatory mortality, it must be remembered, applies to predatory species every bit as much as it does to ducks. A frantic spring/summer campaign followed by a total cessation of hostilities when the new shooting season starts is probably little more than a waste of time.

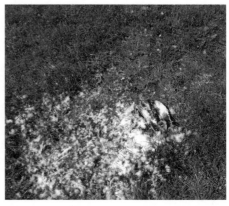

This mallard's head has been removed – evidence of the presence of a mink.

Ducks are vulnerable to peregrines.

Mink tracks   *Fox track*

Sometimes one is only too well aware that there is a major problem. It may be that one comes across a mallard nest full of empty egg shells, a not uncommon event in early spring. Or it may be the headless bodies of young mallard, irrefutable evidence that mink have moved into residence. But, equally, there are periods when there is no such dramatic evidence. Never be complacent though, because these opportunists are rarely absent. And, such is the way of Nature, the more one does to build up stocks of duck the more attractive one's patch becomes for them.

Always therefore be on the look-out for predator calling cards. The pointed tracks of the fox and the star-shaped footprints of mink are quite distinctive. Look for the latter in muddy places along the river bank and in sheltered drains. Get to know the paths they follow because they are creatures of habit. If the grass is long, the fox's path soon becomes apparent. The snare, in my estimation, strategically hung where the path passes through a hedgerow is the best answer to Reynard.

There are activists who are trying to get the snare outlawed. Ridiculous. Properly set up with a swivel and visited regularly, the snare is an efficient and humane method of control. There are various cage-type fox traps on the market but I am not enamoured of them. I have tried every conceivable type of bait in them from rabbit to fish to poultry to steak. Maybe I am doing something wrong but I suspect that the fox is just too cute to go in.

In contrast the cage trap is a certain winner for mink. Mink have favourite coming-ashore points along the river bank and it is here that the trap should be located. Even if there are no footprints around it is worthwhile setting up a trap every couple of weeks or so. Opinions differ widely as to what makes the best bait. My personal preference is for a fresh hind limb of a rabbit, which has rarely let me down. And one small but important point: having captured a mink, despatch it humanely with a .22 rifle. Submerging the trap in order to drown its occupant is neither nice nor humane.

The Larsen trap

For the avian predators the Larsen trap reigns supreme. It will catch the two major egg thieves: the magpie and carrion/hooded crow; as well as such lesser lights as rooks and jackdaws. In theory the trap does its job as a result of introducing a rival into the territory of another. But there is more to it than that. Territorial instincts are pronounced for only part of the year and yet the Larsen trap delivers month after month. I find it especially efficient at picking up young birds. In their case I assume it is a simple matter of curiosity that leads them to their doom. Crows and jackdaws are commonly lured into the trap by a magpie. Again, I assume, curiosity. Strangely it is much rarer to catch a magpie when the decoy is a crow. Maybe magpies are just that wee bit brighter than crows.

From time to time I have heard of a fox, usually a cub, getting caught in a Larsen trap. However until last summer I had never witnessed such an event. I keep a trap in operation for most of the year by our main flight pond. One morning in July I found an almost fully grown fox in one of the catching compartments. The magpie in the middle was viewing it from its perch with rather more than a touch of agitation. It is quite extraordinary how a fox can enter from the top without firing the trap before it is actually inside. My fox was just sitting there looking extremely sad. A friend who had a similar experience captured a rather more resolute fox. It had succeeded in dragging the magpie through the weld mesh and eating it.

Larsen traps are exceedingly simple to operate. There should be at least one in each area in which mallard are known to breed, and not just during the breeding season. As long as the decoy bird has a perch, shelter

Feeding mature mallard at a newly-made lake – a good method of ensuring that ducks return to the same water.

and is well fed and watered it can ply its deadly trade for weeks on end. The magpie that was responsible for the fox's demise was one of the best I ever had. He was credited with the capture of 51 fellow magpies, 16 hooded crows, 5 jackdaws, 1 rook and the fox. It was probably fitting after such sterling service that it escaped courtesy of a moment of clumsiness when one of my sons was putting in a new water container. Remember that when a Larsen trap has stopped catching for a few days, it should be moved to a new location. This need not be very far away. I have on occasions simply relocated one in an adjacent field where it has quickly continued its good work.

Habitat creation

A few words now on the creation of new habitats. Digging out a duck pond is a relatively straightforward matter and one which should be greatly encouraged. It is not my intention here to go into the mechanics of the job because there are a number of excellent publications on the matter. Rather I want to make a few observations that might be of use to anyone thinking of setting about the task. First of all, even a small pond is well worth considering. Properly screened and maintained it can attract a surprising number of ducks. Location is most likely to be dictated by topography.

If one has a small river or even a stream, there is enormous potential for a pond. An ideal situation arises where a ditch separating two fields meets a stream. A pond can be cut in the angle between the ditch and the stream in either or both fields with minimal loss of land. We recently developed one like this. The water surface barely exceeds one hundred square yards yet the pond delivers a satisfactory flight every few weeks. Last season we accounted for exactly forty mallard there, all wild birds. A bonus of this location is that the vegetation on the ditch overhangs the pond, providing shelter and, in the summer, a good supply of insects for the ducklings that hatch in the vicinity. The nests are usually some distance away but the mothers bring their broods to the pond within hours of hatching.

Another advantage of digging a pond out from an adjoining stream is that it retains moving water during frosty periods and can thus be very attractive to ducks. Other locations that can be exploited for pond digging include boggy areas where the water table is not too far beneath the surface or hollows into which it is possible to divert water. I know of one man who deepened a hollow about one hundred yards behind his farmyard and piped all the rainwater from the roofs of his sheds into it.

Since the object of the exercise is mainly to attract dabbling ducks, the pond should be quite shallow. A couple of feet is more than sufficient. Should there be diving ducks in the area it might be worth considering deepening one side in the hope of attracting them. I have dug out a pond like this at the back of our farm. It falls away from a depth of two feet at one end to approximately five at the other end. I have to confess however that diving ducks have yet to take it seriously. To date only a solitary tufted duck has joined the mallard and teal there.

Conventional wisdom has it that the banks should be gently sloped to provide loafing areas. The pond is then fed in the adjoining shallows.

I cannot however agree that this is always the best design, especially if the pond is to be used for release purposes. Unless the regime of predator control is very efficient or the pond is securely fenced, providing roosting quarters at the edge can be a recipe for disaster. Young released mallard can be naive in the extreme and foxes will not take long to discover their presence.

My preference is to have steep sides to discourage the young birds from coming out. Some do of course insist on doing just that but it is not a major problem, because we have fashioned a large island in each of the ponds. The banks of the islands are sloped gently and from day one we feed the ducks on these banks. Thus they get used to using the islands and spend much of their time loafing on them. It is a little tedious to don waders every time in order to wade across to feed the islands but the eventual return is well worth the effort. Once the ducks are flying well we no longer need to cross to the islands. Instead barley is broadcast in the shallows.

Pond-feeding

Finally, in relation to feeding, two questions remain. How often should a pond be fed? And is all-year-round feeding a good idea?

When our new supply of six-week-olds arrives in early July, I make a point of feeding them around dusk and dawn for the first few days. This is because our main release pond is located in a very wild and lonesome spot where there are rather more predators than we would like. The more that the new arrivals can be encouraged to spend time on the island, the better, especially during the hours of darkness. As soon as possible however, I drop the morning feed so as not to develop a culture of over-dependency. Thereafter they are fed every evening until they are flying well and moving out to nearby stubbles. At this juncture, feeding is reduced to three times a week, a procedure which is maintained until the end of the shooting season. It is important to keep feeding on a regular basis because mallard can fairly quickly relocate if deprived of their 'fix' of barley for any length of time.

As to all-year-round feeding, I have to confess to a certain degree of ambivalence. It can, on the one hand, be argued that to continue feeding after the close of the shooting season is a waste of good barley. And, furthermore, it is bound to attract unpaired drakes which are more than likely to disturb breeding birds. On the other hand, feeding will help to ensure that breeding birds remain in the area and, it is hoped, rear a few good broods.

Of recent years, I have opted for light feeding a couple of times a week from the close of the season to the arrival of the new stock. This has certainly resulted in more broods appearing on the pond than was the case when we stopped feeding on 31st January. Disappointingly though, in quite a lot of cases the duck insists on taking her brood to the river (some half mile away) when the ducklings are only a few days old. Extra feeding at this juncture does not seem to make any difference. I do not know if there is any solution to this particular problem, short of fencing off each pond, something I have little inclination to do.

That's about it so. Wishful thinking perhaps, but I'd like to hope that, in some small way, these pages will help to promote the cause of those wild and wonderful creatures of the wet places, and of the sport that they provide.

References

Bellrose, F.C. *Lead poisoning as a mortality factor in waterfowl populations,* 1959. Illinois Nat. His. Surv. Bull. 27; 235–288.

Butler, D. *The incidence of lead shot ingestion in wildfowl in Ireland,* 1990. Irish Naturalists Journal Vol. 23, No.8; 309–313.

Grinnell, G.B. *American Duck Shooting,* 1901. 1991 edition, Stackpole Books, Harrisburg.

Heaton, A. *Duck Decoys,* 2001. Shire Publications Ltd., Princes Risborough.

Hill, D.A. *Population Regulation in the Mallard* (Anas Platyrhyncos) 1984. The Journal of Animal Ecology, Vol. 53 No. 1; 191–202.

Hutchinson, C. *Ireland's Wetlands and their Birds,* 1979. Irish Wildbird Conservancy, Dublin.

Hutchinson, C. *Birds in Ireland,* 1989. T. and A.D. Poyser Ltd, Calton.

Lack, P. *Atlas of Wintering Birds in Britain and Ireland,* 1986. T. and A. D. Poyser Ltd., Calton.

Marchington, J. *The History of Wildfowling,* 1980. A & C Black, London.

Migratory Birds Convention Act 1984. Canada, 2005

Mudge, S. and Burn, H. *Wildfowl,* 1988. Christopher Helm, London.

Nichols, J.D., Johnson, F.A. and Williams, B.K. *Managing North American Waterfowl Populations in the Face of Uncertainty,* 1995. Annual Review of Ecology and Systematics, Vol 26; 177–199.

Owen, M., Atkinson–Willes and Salmon, D. *Wildfowl in Great Britain* (2nd edition), 1986. C.U.P.

Parkes, C. and Thornley, J. *Fair Game. The Law of Country Sports and the Protection of Wildlife*, 1994. Pelham Books, London.

Sharrock, J.T.R. *The Atlas of Breeding Birds in Britain and Ireland*, 4th Impression, 1987.

Soothill, E. and Whitehead, P. *Wildfowl of the World*, 1978. Blandford Press Ltd., Poole.

U.S. Fish and Wildlife Service, *Waterfowl Population Status*, 2005.

Useful Organisations & Addresses

British Association for Shooting & Conservation (BASC)
www.basc.org.uk
Tel: 01244 573000 (Wildfowling: 01244 573011)

U.S. Fish and Wildlife Service
Migratory Bird Program: **www.fws.gov/migratorybirds**

American Waterfowl Population Status Report
www.fws.gov/migratorybirds/NewReportsPublications/Popula
tionStatus/Waterfowl/StatusReport2009.Final.pdf

Ducks Unlimited (USA)
www.ducks.org   Tel: 901-758-3825

Flyways.US
Waterfowl hunting management in North America: **www.flyway.us**

US Geological Survey – Ducks at a Distance
A waterfowl identification guide: **www.npwrc.usgs.gov**

Waterfowler.com (USA)
For real-time hunting reports, state by state
www.waterfowler.com

Canadian Wildlife Service
National Wildlife Research Centre: Bird Banding Office
For information about migratory bird populations in Canada
www.cws-scf.ec.gc.ca

Many of the shooting periodicals on both sides of the Atlantic carry advertisements and information sections on duck shooting holidays (vacations). These, and various promotional websites, are probably the best sources for ideas and practical advice on the subject.

Index

Also published by Merlin Unwin Books

www.merlinunwin.co.uk
(00 44) +1584 877456

Rough Shooting in Ireland
Douglas Butler £20 ISBN 9781873674895

Geese! Memoirs of a Wildfowler
Edward Miller £20 ISBN 9781873674130

The Shootingman's Bedside Book
an anthology compiled by BB £18.95 ISBN 9781873674666

That Strange Alchemy
Pheasants, Trout and a Middle-Aged Man
Laurence Catlow £17.99 ISBN 9781906122034

The Poacher's Handbook
Ian Niall £14.95 ISBN 9781873674581

The Poacher's Cookbook
Prue Coats £11.99 ISBN 9781873674611

Private Thoughts from a Small Shoot
Laurence Catlow £17.99 ISBN 9781873674680

Advice from a Gamekeeper
John Cowan £20 ISBN 9781906122119

Apley Hall
The Golden Years of a Sporting Estate
Norman Sharpe £12 ISBN 9781906122164

Manual of a Traditional Bacon Curer
Maynard Davies £25 ISBN 9781906122089